THERESA REBECK
Complete Plays Volume III

Short Plays 1989–2005

THERESA REBECK

Complete Plays Volume III
Short Plays 1989–2005

CONTEMPORARY PLAYWRIGHTS
SERIES

A Smith and Kraus Book

A Smith and Kraus Book
Published by Smith and Kraus, Inc.
177 Lyme Road, Hanover, New Hampshire, 03755
www.smithandkraus.com

First Edition: June 2007
10 9 8 7 6 5 4 3 2 1
Manufactured in the United States of America
Cover and text design by Julia Hill Gignoux, Freedom Hill Design
Cover image: Austin Lysy and Kate Burton in The Water's Edge. *Photo by Joan Marcus.*

The Library of Congress Cataloging-In-Publication Data
Rebeck, Theresa.
[Plays]
Theresa Rebeck: collected plays. —1st ed.
p. cm. — (Contemporary playwrights series)
ISBN-10 1-57525-447-6 / ISBN-13 978-1-57525-447-0
I. Title. II. Series.
PS3568.E2697A19 1998
812'.54—dc21 98-53027

CONTENTS

FOR KATE SNODGRASS
ALSO KNOWN AS KATHERINE, KATHY, BITSY, AND "PIG,"
BUT ALWAYS AND EVER MISS KATE TO ME.

INTRODUCTION

For the contemporary playwright, short plays too often become the forgotten jewels of a body of work. How ironic, then, that short plays have countless opportunities to be created for today's theater. Some are written "on demand" for wild events like New York's "The 24 Hour Plays" where, as the name suggests, new short plays are created, cast, and staged within one day. Others are solicited by contests like the Humana Festival of New American Plays in Louisville, Kentucky. Still others are submitted to theaters across the country for showcases of hot playwrights. And while this output is sometimes anthologized, it is too often lost in the capricious stream of a culture that perpetually demands something new.

I've been fortunate to personally know Theresa Rebeck for many years. But I have known of her by reputation for even longer. As a fellow graduate of Brandeis University, I heard of the "savagely funny" Theresa before I read one of her plays or before she found the success she has justifiably earned. Her presence permeated the campus even though we were in different programs (and separated by a few years). Such is the indelible impression Theresa always makes. Her vision is both unique and universal, her writing is ferocious, and her work — as I can now personally attest — is "savagely funny."

Working in the professional theater I've found a new way that Theresa's work surrounds me. Each season I sit through long days of open auditions where actors bring in their favorite monologues. Fifteen or so years ago, young actors favored Lanford Wilson, Wendy Wasserstein, Chris Durang, and Beth Henley. And while these contemporary writers have remained perennial favorites, I've noticed a marked change in the material actors select. Now, my days are filled with a procession of the plays of Theresa Rebeck: *Loose Knit, Family of Mann,* and *Spike Heels,* to name a few. Many actors, so eager to embrace her writing, often seek out her plays before they are even published; recently, I listened to several monologues from *The Water's Edge* several months before it was produced by Second Stage Theatre. It is usually women who prepare these monologues because Theresa has become cherished as a writer who creates strong, visceral, and unforgettable women's roles. As anyone familiar with her work could tell you, Theresa's writing is just as fascinating and compelling for men, and this collection of short plays is no exception.

In the theater community, Theresa is known as a generous artist who has contributed blistering short work for many of the programs mentioned earlier. Theresa has said that short plays should be just as fulfilling, challenging, and complex as longer pieces. The work in this volume clearly demonstrates her belief.

For the first time, Theresa's short plays are published as a single collection. It is very exciting that this work is now available to future generations of actors, directors, and theater companies. The collection reveals a mind carefully attuned to the rhythms of our society and a deep understanding of the personal obstacles individuals face. I have no doubt that these plays will become the staple of acting classes across the country. I am also certain that I will hear these pieces in auditions for years to come.

Christopher Burney
Associate Artistic Director
Second Stage Theatre

WHAT WE'RE UP AGAINST

CHARACTERS
STU: White, thirty
BEN: White, thirty

SET
An office

ORIGINAL PRODUCTION
What We're Up Against was originally produced at Naked Angels in the spring of 1992, Suzanne Brinkley, director, with the following cast:

STU . . . . .Fisher Stevens
BEN . . . . .Billy Strong

Stu and Ben sit at a drafting table. Stu reaches into the bottom drawer of a file cabinet, finds a bottle of scotch, and pours drinks.

STU: All I'm saying is there's —

BEN: Rules. That's what I'm trying to —

STU: A *sys*tem.

BEN: Yes, Jesus, I —

STU: Things don't just happen, history, events —

BEN: I know, this is not —

STU: We *create.*

BEN: Exactly. A company. I tried to —

STU: You look at anything, the Boy Scouts, some fucking *convent,* and maybe it doesn't seem like —

BEN: You just can't —

STU: It's part of something much more *com*plicated. You can't just act like that's not true.

BEN: That's my point. She's a fucking bitch. That's all I'm saying.

STU: I'm not *saying* that. That is not what —

BEN: OK, OK, fine, but —

STU: You cannot give them that.

BEN: I'm not giving them anything. I'm just saying, she doesn't belong. I don't know why they hired another fucking woman, it's not like —

STU: Look, they want to work, women want to work, they should have the opportunity. I'm not saying — fuck, that's just — you know that's what they think, they all have their little meetings and tell each other that we don't *want* them, we're *threat*ened, when that's not the issue. You can't give them that. Because that's not the problem.

BEN: Stu, you just said she —

STU: She *tricked* me. The bitch tricked me, that is my point. She is a lying, deceitful, dishonest little manipulator. I don't mind working with her. But, she is a cunt. That, I mind.

BEN: That's what I'm —

STU: No, that is not what you're saying, Ben. These are two very different things. I welcomed her. I was happy when they hired her, I said, I want to work with this woman.

BEN: Oh, come on —

STU: Excuse me?

BEN: What? I'm just saying —

STU: What are you saying, Ben?

BEN: I'm *saying*, shit, I'm saying you didn't want her any more than the rest of us. What do we need another woman for? Janice is, we have one of them, I don't know what —

STU: This isn't an issue of sex. That's what I'm telling you. Are you fucking listening to me?

BEN: Yes, I'm listening, you're not —

STU: It's the system I'm talking about. It's not whether or not she's a *woman*. It's the fact that she has no re*spect,* this is my point. She comes into my office and says, we need to talk, Stu, and I'm, OK, I'm fine, I can talk, I don't have a problem with this. She has questions. I'm fine with this. She wants to know why I won't let her work. Now, that is not what is happening, I explain that to her. She is a new employee, how long has she been here, five months, six months, this is not — the experience isn't there. That is my point. When the experience is there, she'll be put on projects. She wants to know how she can get the experience if we won't let her work. This is a good question. And so I tell her: initiative. Initiative, that is how the system works, that is how America works, this is what they don't under*stand.* No one *hands* you things. You *work* for them. You *earn* them. You prove yourself *worthy.* So she says to me, what about Webber? And I say, what about him? And she says, you let him work. He's been here four months, and you put him on projects.

BEN: Oh, that fucking —

STU: Exactly. She's jealous. The bitch is jealous. She doesn't care about the work, she just cares, she's competitive, Webber got ahead of her and she doesn't like it. She's after his balls. So I say to her, that's got nothing to do with you. Nothing. This isn't about competition. This is about business. We use the best person for the job. If you prove yourself, through initiative, to be the best person, to be *worthy,* we will use you.

BEN: So what'd she say to —

STU: I'll tell you what she said. This fucking bitch, she stopped by Webber's office and picked up a copy of that mall extension you guys are working on, the Roxbury project —

BEN: What? What'd she do that for?

STU: So she's got your design, right —

BEN: That thing's not finished, Stu. Did she show you that? She had no business doing that. We are not finished with that.

STU: So she says to me —

BEN: I cannot believe that bitch, trying to make us look bad! We haven't solved the duct thing yet, OK, we're still working on it! I can't be*lieve* —

STU: Would you shut up, Ben? I'm trying to ex*plain* something to you. She's not after your balls, she's after Webber —

BEN: I'm just saying, we're still working on that. We've got *ideas*.

STU: I'm not talking about your *ideas,* Ben, I'm trying to tell you something! She brings me your design, she tells me she got it from Webber, and then she says, I can see putting Ben on this, he's got se*nior*ity. But why does Webber get to work, and not me? What is so good about what he does? Tell me why Webber got this project and not me. She's pissing me off now, because I explained this to her, it's not about competition, I *said* that, but if she wants to play this game, fine, *fuck* her, I'll *show* her why Webber got the project. So I go through it. Every detail. I show her how every fucking detail indicates that Webber has experience. I prove it to her. And you know what she says to me? "I designed that."

BEN: What?

STU: The bitch put Webber's name on one of her designs. She came up with her own fucking design for that fucking mall, and then she pretended it was Webber's. She tricked me.

BEN: You're shitting me.

STU: This fucking *woman* stands there — she stands there, and says to me, "This is my point, *Stu.* It's not about the work, it's about point of view. When a woman designs it, it's shit, and when a man designs it, it's great." So I say to her, no this isn't about point of view, this is about power, you fucking bitch. You're trying to cut off my balls here. She says, look at the design, Stu, you know it's good, and I say, I don't give a shit if it's good. You want to play by these rules, I can play by these rules. It's shit. Get out of my face.

BEN: You said that?

STU: She says, I want to work. Why won't you let me work? And I say fuck you. What you want is power. You fucking cunt, don't lie to me. You come in here and try and cut off my balls, I welcomed you, and this is what you do.

BEN: Fucking bitch.

STU: This is what we're up against.

BEN: Fuck.

(Pause. They think about this.)

BEN: But it was good?

STU: What?

BEN: The design. You said —

STU: Fuck you, are you fucking listening to a word I'm saying?

BEN: Yes, I'm listening, I just — I was wondering what she did with the air ducts.

STU: What? What are you saying?

BEN: I'm saying, you know, Webber and I — those fucking ducts are all over the entryway there, and we can't —

STU: Fuck you, Ben, you are not listening to a word out of my mouth.

BEN: Yeah, I know, she's a cunt, I'm just saying, you said the design was good, so I was just wondering —

STU: The design is shit.

BEN: Yeah, but if she's got an idea —

STU: She's got nothing, Ben. *Nothing.* You give her nothing.

BEN: Why not?

STU: Excuse me? What? Excuse me?

BEN: If she's got one fucking idea —

STU: She *tricked* me.

BEN: Yeah, but you don't let her work, Stu. She's right about that. You let Janice do more, and her work is for shit.

STU: What are you — what is your fucking point, Ben?

BEN: I don't have a point! I just want to see that fucking design. Webber and I have been going over that fucking duct thing for weeks and we can't crack it. So, if she's got a solution, I want to see it. Did she have a solution or not?

STU: Yeah. She did.

BEN: Well, I want to see it.

STU: No.

BEN: She's here now, fuck, they hired her and we had nothing to say about it, she's being paid, why shouldn't we use her?

STU: I'll tell you why. Because then, she's won. She didn't wait. She didn't play by the rules. It's context. If she had waited, it would've been different. If she had respect for the system. But she has no respect. This is what we're up against.

BEN: That's a load of shit, Stu.

STU: I'm what? Excuse me, did you, what did you —

BEN: Look, Stu —

STU: If she were here, listening to us, you know what she'd do?

BEN: Hopefully, she'd tell me what she did with those fucking ducts —

STU: No. That is not what she'd do. I'll tell you what she'd do. Two men, having a simple conversation, we're having drinks. Right? Is there anything wrong with this? But she sits here and she listens to us, and then she goes and tells her little friends. She goes back to her little group, and she says,

"They said this, and they said that, they called me a bitch, they called me a cunt" and she and her friends, they all act like this is some big fucking *point*. But there is no *point*, Ben. This is what they don't understand. There is a system. Things fit together. It's not about point of view. It's just about the way things are. They want things to be the way they're not. They don't get it, and they're trying to make us pay for that. But they are not going to win. It's the system. That's all it is. The system. *(They stare at each other. Blackout.)*

END OF PLAY

KATIE AND FRANK

CHARACTERS

KATIE: Early thirties, scattered, angry, but not crazy
FRANK: Early thirties, on his own track

SET

A room with a bed or a couch or a chair, a door, and a phone. The door leads to the bathroom.

ORIGINAL PRODUCTION

Katie and Frank was originally produced at Naked Angels West in June 1996, Geoffrey Nauffts, director, with the following cast:

KATIE . . . . .Laura Selvato
FRANK . . . . .Tim Ransom

Katie lies on the bed. Frank is in and out of the bathroom.

KATIE: I talked to your mother the other day.

FRANK: *(Offstage.)* What?

KATIE: Your mother called yesterday.

FRANK: Oh yeah? *(He crosses through, wearing an open shirt and nice trousers. He is absurdly handsome.)*

KATIE: I told you. Last night.

FRANK: No you didn't.

KATIE: Yes, I did, remember, after you got home from work, I said —

FRANK: I don't remember.

KATIE: It was just yesterday.

FRANK: I don't remember.

KATIE: It was —

FRANK: Katie. I don't remember.

(Having found his socks he returns to the bathroom. She lies on the bed, thinking.)

KATIE: It was after therapy. I remember telling you because I was so upset, I mean, I came from therapy, I was feeling *good*, you know, I was just feeling, sitting here feeling good for a change and then your fucking mother called.

FRANK: *(Offstage.)* That's nice. That's very nice

KATIE: Well, I told you to call her and you didn't. The last time? Whenever that was, last week, and I told you to call her but you didn't so then she called me yesterday to scream at me. *(Suddenly loud.)* AND I TOLD YOU THIS LAST NIGHT AND NOW YOU'RE SAYING YOU DON'T REMEMBER.

(Frank appears in the doorway, annoyed.)

FRANK: Katie. Do you mind? I'm about to walk out the door here and I don't have time for one of your whatever these things are.

KATIE: Where are you going?

FRANK: *(Offstage.)* Work.

KATIE: It's Saturday.

FRANK: *(Offstage.)* I work on Saturdays.

KATIE: Yeah, so you say.

FRANK: Katie, please!

KATIE: *(To herself.)* Yeah, fuck you, Frank. Why don't you call your fucking mother for once?

(Frank appears.)

FRANK: I mean, I thought you were feeling better. I mean, you said, a minute ago, that after therapy yesterday, you felt better. Did you not say that?

KATIE: Yes I did. I did feel better. But —

FRANK: So why don't you hang onto that? Huh? I just don't — your life is not some huge fucking torture here. I don't know why it always has to be like this.

KATIE: Well, I'll tell you why it has to be like this. It has to be like this because you won't call your mother.

FRANK: I can't talk to you when you're like this.

KATIE: This is my point! This is my whole point! Why don't you call your mother? You know when you don't call her she blames it all on me, and then I end up taking endless hours of shit from her on the phone. Is he there? Well why didn't he call me? Did you tell him? I just don't understand why if you told him he doesn't call. Like it's my fault, you know, God forbid it should ever be *your* fault. It's just, why don't you tell her? Why don't you ever call her and say I'm sorry I forgot to call. Katie told me you called but I *forgot*. That's all I'm *saying*.

FRANK: You're going to drive me nuts.

(He crosses through, truly annoyed, finds his tie and exits again. Katie watches him.)

KATIE: *(Sad, to herself.)* I just don't understand why it's all my fault. *(Beat. Quiet.)* My therapist says you don't listen to me.

FRANK: *(Out of the bathroom like a shot.)* Oh, no. No no no. That's the one thing I said to you, when you went into therapy, I will pay for this, but I will not be *blamed*. You are not dumping all your problems on me. That is not an option here.

KATIE: I didn't —

FRANK: It's not an option, Katie! *(He goes back into the bathroom.)*

(Beat.)

KATIE: I bought a gun.

(Frank sticks his head out, looks at her.)

KATIE: *(Innocent.)* What?

FRANK: *(Disgusted.)* Nothing. Nothing. *(He goes back in the bathroom.)*

KATIE: I did. This morning. I went out and bought a gun. It's absurdly easy, you know, you walk into a store and just, like, buy it. Actually, you go in on Monday and pay for it but they don't give it to you until today because of this *waiting* period, they make you wait before they give you the gun just in case you want to change your *mind*, like they think if some woman comes in here going you know, I hate my husband, I think

I'll just put a bullet between his eyes, that they need to give her a few days to consider that. Which doesn't seem like great logic to me, frankly. If you're thinking about shooting your husband it seems to me an extra week is just going to make you more determined to do it. Unless that's what they're hoping for.

FRANK: *(Entering.)* Where's the toothpaste?

KATIE: We're out.

FRANK: We're out.

KATIE: No, wait, there's some in that little, one of those travel things I put together. The blue thing in the back of the towels.

(He glares at her pointedly for a moment, and goes.)

KATIE: So anyway, this gun —

FRANK: *(Offstage.)* I can't find it!

KATIE: It's in the blue thing!

FRANK: I TOLD YOU, I CAN'T — *(Silence.)* Never mind.

(Silence. She continues.)

KATIE: I could have gotten more than one, you know. They make you wait, but you can buy as many as you want. I asked the guy about it. I said, if I wanted to buy like, eleven guns or something wouldn't you worry about that? Wouldn't that seem kind of hostile to you? And he said it was my right. To buy that many guns. Like that made it OK.

(She is vaguely bemused by this. Frank appears in the doorway.)

FRANK: This is ridiculous you know. This toothpaste situation? I mean, I'm just squeezing here, for this *squidge,* it's not even, when was the last time you went to the store? I understand that you're *troubled* but I don't think it's asking too much that you occasionally get it together to go to the store and buy a fucking tube of toothpaste. All right? I do not raise my voice to you, but I feel a little strongly about this.

(He exits again. She reaches under the bed and gets her purse. She pulls out a gun.)

KATIE: So anyway I have this gun because it's my *right*. Which means, I think, that's it's probably my right to shoot you. Because OK this is why: It's my right to buy a gun, I buy a gun because I hate my husband, it's my right to hate my husband because well we don't need to go into that but let's just say the reasons are VERY CLEAR therefore, it's my right to shoot my husband. What's that called? A logical syllogism. I think therefore I am. I hate you and therefore we are. Therefore you're dead you lying fucking bastard, you lying fuckface, you liar liar liar —

FRANK: This isn't funny, Katie. *(He appears in the door, tying his tie. He sees the gun and stops.)* What's that?

KATIE: I told you. I bought a gun.

FRANK: That's not a gun.

KATIE: I told you, Frank. They'll sell a gun to any idiot who asks for one. Did I not just tell you this? Do you listen to a word out of my mouth? This is what my therapist says —

FRANK: Hey —

KATIE: No, this is just what she's talking about, and then you *complain,* you say I'm *blaming* you when it's the truth. YOU DON'T LISTEN.

FRANK: Katie, put the gun down.

KATIE: I'm not going to put it down. I just got it. It's brand-new. I'm getting used to it. I like the way it makes me feel. It's my right to feel this way.

FRANK: I'm calling your useless therapist —

(He starts to move for the phone. She points it at him.)

KATIE: Oh now you're calling her. I asked you, I *asked* you to go with me and you couldn't be bothered because she's a fucking idiot, but now you want to talk to her because I have a gun is that it?

FRANK: Katie, you're clearly losing it.

KATIE: Gee Frank I wonder why that is. *(Beat.)* Anyway, it doesn't matter. I can be completely fucking out of my fucking mind and it's still my right to own a gun, and it's my right to point it at you and it's my right to feel what I feel. Some country, America. *(She has the gun right up against his head.)*

FRANK: *(Really scared now.)* Katie. Katie.

KATIE: What Frank?

FRANK: Come on, honey. Put the gun down.

KATIE: Frank. This is the first time you've listened to me in years. Why would I put the gun down?

FRANK: Honey —

KATIE: Honey. That's a good one.

FRANK: What do you want, Katie? What do you want?

KATIE: *(Beat.)* I want you to call your mother, Frank. And I want you to say, Mom, how are you? Katie told me you called, and I forgot to call you back.

FRANK: *(Resisting.)* Katie —

KATIE: Pick up the phone. *(The gun goes to his head again.)* Pick up the phone, Frank.

(He does. Blackout.)

END OF PLAY

THE CONTRACT

CHARACTERS
 PHIL: An agent
 TOM: An actor

SET
 An agent's office

ORIGINAL PRODUCTION
 The Contract was originally produced at Naked Angels West in July
 1996, Jerry Levine, director, with the following cast:

 PHIL ....Merrill Holtzman
 TOM ....Willy Gerson

Two men sit in an office. Phil sits at a desk, reading Tom's résumé.

PHIL: Yeah, this is —

TOM: I also dance. Plus, I condensed. That's not everything.

PHIL: Oh —

TOM: I mean, it's representative. There's a ton more stuff, I just thought —

PHIL: No question. The thing is, your type —

TOM: I don't really see myself as a type. There's much more range, you know different —

PHIL: Character —

TOM: Yeah, character-type work, and, um, improvisation —

PHIL: This is what I'm saying. A character actor, what are you, mid-thirties —

TOM: Early. Early thirties, although I often read, last year, I played a twenty-three-year-old junkie, in an independent, and it was —

PHIL: *(Slightly impressed.)* A junkie? 'Cause there's maybe, they're hot this year —

TOM: You want tape on that? 'Cause I could get you that tape. The junkie tape —

PHIL: Yeah, I —

TOM: I mean, it was excellent, I didn't have a lot to do, but there's a great cameo of me nodding off, it's killer stuff —

PHIL: No, you know what you should do? All this, you do a lot of theater, right? This is mostly like stage stuff?

TOM: Yeah, a lot, my training is —

PHIL: Fantastic. I love the theater. Why don't you give us a call, next time you're in something, we'll stop by and take a look, OK?
(He pushes the résumé toward Tom. Tom does not take it.)

TOM: Well but isn't that why you called me in? 'Cause you saw the showcase and —

PHIL: It would just be great to see you in something bigger. Get more of a sense of what you can do.

TOM: Yeah but you called and asked me to come in and now —

PHIL: Hey can I be candid? *(Looks at résumé.)* Tom? I mean, this is a tough business, it's best to be candid, right?

TOM: Oh absolutely, that's —

PHIL: 'Cause I'm sort of not really getting your tone here. I mean I called you in 'cause I think you have talent, I might want to, you know, *represent* you someday and now I'm getting like a ton of attitude here.

TOM: No, you're not getting attitude. I just —

PHIL: I'm just saying. Don't talk to me like a jerk.

TOM: I'm not talking to you like a jerk. You're talking to me like — You call me in, I take time out of my schedule —

PHIL: Your very busy schedule — *(He waves the résumé, unimpressed.)*

TOM: I told you, that's not — besides, who cares what's on my — Harrison Ford was a *carpenter* for God's sake —

PHIL: If you were Harrison Ford, believe me, this conversation would be very different.

TOM: You called me. *You* called *me* —

PHIL: Yes, I called you and you jumped. You jumped at this. I mean, you want representation or not? You want it or not?

TOM: Of course I want it, I —

PHIL: All right. I am the representation. I am what you want. I am the object of desire in this town. Got that? It's not some fucking starlet tits out to here. It isn't a gold BMW. It's me. You want to work, you want to see your face on the big screen, the fucking tube, whatever —

TOM: Look, I —

PHIL: *(Very reasonable.)* I am what gets you that. I am what makes this town run. So when I say jump, you don't say why. I mean, what, you have a problem with authority? You didn't like your dad or something? Tell it to your shrink. Keep it out of my damn office and just do what I say.

TOM: Why are you yelling at me?

PHIL: Oh, now I'm —

TOM: Yes, you're not even representing me and you're, you're —

PHIL: I said I *might.*

TOM: Oh well that's —

PHIL: Look. I didn't invent the world. I didn't make up the rules. I'm giving you advice here. This is free! Do you know what you are? You're an actor! No one gives a shit about you! You're a total nobody! The fact that I'm even speaking to you is going to be the most significant thing that happens to you all year. You should be fucking genuflecting, and I mean literally hitting your knees when I say boo, and what do I get instead? What do I *get?* "You called me up and now you aren't being nice to me." This is show business, you moron! Nobody's nice to anybody! Especially actors. You guys are the lowest form of life. Oh yeah, I know everybody says that about agents, but they're wrong. I mean, we're slime, OK, I don't argue that, but we're slime that *you* need, and *you* want, so you are lower even than me, and that means I don't *have* to be nice to you. *You* have to be nice to me!

TOM: I just — I don't — that's nuts. You're nuts.

PHIL: I'm *what?*

TOM: I mean, I'm an actor. How can you — I'm an *artist.* Laurence Olivier, for God's sake — this is an art form and you're — yeah, OK, I understand that it's not show friends, it's show business, but — we're talking about telling *stories,* reaching in and communicating our hu*man*ity, and if you can't even — if decency means *nothing* anymore, then why — I just don't accept that. I'm sorry, but I don't. I've given up everything to do this work, my family thinks I'm completely — I've maxed out all — I mean, I am fucking broke every second of my life, and I know that I'm just another actor but that's not — this is a *noble thing.* Do you understand that? We are as puppets dancing for the gods. We spin meaning out of nothing, out of oblivion we make *art,* and you — well. You're not — I can't — you don't — No.

PHIL: Did you finish a sentence in there? I mean, did you actually say something?

TOM: I don't want you to represent me.

PHIL: You *what?*

TOM: You're a bad person. *(Tom takes his résumé and puts it in his knapsack.)*

PHIL: Oh. Well. You cut me to the quick, Tom. I, I just don't know what to say.

(Tom is heading for the door.)

PHIL: Hey! What are you doing?

TOM: I'm leaving.

PHIL: Did I say you could go? 'Cause I don't remember saying that.

TOM: I, I didn't ask.

PHIL: Tom. This is really — sit down. Would you sit down? Come on. I mean, I like you Tom, would I be even talking to you if I didn't — sit down. Come on.

(Tom does.)

TOM: I'm really confused.

PHIL: I don't see why.

TOM: I'm getting very mixed signals from you.

PHIL: How so, Tom? 'Cause I'm being as candid as I possibly know how to be. I mean, most people in this town — some of that stuff you said, you could've really pissed some people off with that. And you know, someone like me, if I were vindictive, I could call every casting agent I know and tell them, you know, you're a difficult guy, and that would be it. Your career would be over.

TOM: Is that a threat?

PHIL: It's just a fact. Nobody wants to deal with anybody who's difficult. Life's too short, babe. You want to have a conversation about, what do you call it —

TOM: The work?

PHIL: "The work," people aren't gonna put up with that. Humanity, noble, decency, art — Tom. People are not gonna put up with it.

TOM: Why are you saying these things? I was going to leave. I am leaving — *(He stands.)*

PHIL: You leave when I tell you to leave!
(Tom looks at him, confused.)

PHIL: I mean, there's something you're not getting here, Tom. I am your friend. I see an actor with talent, I ask him to come in, he's clearly confused about how the world works but I like him so I decide to teach him a few useful lessons. I am your friend. And if you ever want to work as an actor, get paid, actually have a real acting job instead of some stupid *theater* thing, then you will LEAVE when I SAY LEAVE.
(They stare at each other.)

TOM: You know, Nietzsche was not right.

PHIL: Oh, Jesus —

TOM: Yes, Nietzsche, the philosopher said —

PHIL: I'm trying to tell you something, Tom —

TOM: And I'm trying to tell you, the guy was like obsessed —

PHIL: Yeah, that's fascinating, I'm so —

TOM: So we did this acting exercise in grad school, which was based on a Nietzschean model of humanity and basically the exercise was all about who's going to win the scene, because Nietzsche has this theory about the will to power but —

PHIL: DON'T YOU FUCKING TALK TO ME ABOUT NIETZSCHE!

TOM: *(Cowed but continuing.)* It's just that it's a very limited model of humanity. As an actor you have to draw on many aspects of . . . you know what? I can see that this is really important to you, so you know what I'm going to do? I'm going to let you win the scene. *(He sits back down.)*

PHIL: You're what?

TOM: Whatever you want, Phil. I'll do whatever you want. You want me to stay, leave, whatever. That's what I'll do.

PHIL: I want you to listen.

TOM: I'm listening.

PHIL: I want you to get with the picture.

TOM: That's what I'm doing.

PHIL: I mean, which one of us knows this town, you or me?

TOM: You.

PHIL: That's right.

TOM: That's right. And I really appreciate everything you've said to me. You really put me on the right path and I appreciate it.

PHIL: You should.

TOM: I do.

(Tom looks at him. Phil studies him, uncomfortable.)

PHIL: What are you doing?

TOM: I'm letting you win the scene.

PHIL: You're *letting* me? What do you mean, you're —

TOM: I don't mean anything.

PHIL: You said "let."

TOM: That's not what I meant at all. What I meant was it just took me a while to understand what you were trying to tell me, and I'm just, I'm saying you're right. You are right. You're amazing. It's a thrill meeting you and thank you for your time.

PHIL: *(Suspicious.)* You're acting, aren't you?

TOM: Do you want me to be acting?

PHIL: Yeah, that's funny. I mean, you're a real comedian.

TOM: If that's what you want me to be.

(He strikes a little shticky pose for him. Phil laughs a little. Tom joins him. They have a good chuckle together. Phil looks at him, liking him again.)

PHIL: So . . . was this whole thing an act? One big mind-fuck? Nietzsche and art and humanity — you been putting the whole thing on, right? You're fucking with my head so I'll sign you. Am I right? I mean, 'cause that's kind of brilliant.

TOM: Well . . .

PHIL: I mean, I could work with that. 'Cause then we understand each other. You know, then we're on a wavelength.

TOM: *(Some growing concern.)* Oh . . . oh. Oh, oh, oh.

PHIL: *(Snapping again.)* Oh what? Are we understanding each other or not? I mean, am I winning this scene or not?

TOM: Yeah. Yeah, of course.

(Phil studies Tom, then points his finger at him and starts laughing. Tom laughs too, a bit uncomfortably.)

PHIL: I like you. I like you. *(He thinks for a minute, then suddenly yells.)* Hey SUZIE! Get me a set of standard contracts, will you?

(Tom looks around, concerned.)

TOM: Oh. You want to —

PHIL: I'm gonna sign you, Tom! Welcome to Hollywood.

(He shakes his hand, laughing. Tom laughs too. The laughter goes on for quite a while. Tom ends up looking a little sick.)

(Blackout.)

END OF PLAY

SEX WITH THE CENSOR

CHARACTERS
WOMAN: A prostitute
MAN: The censor

SET
A bare room. A small cot covered with a bedspread has been set to one side. There is also a chair.

ORIGINAL PRODUCTION
Sex with the Censor was originally produced at Naked Angels in June 1990, Jace Alexander, director, with the following cast:

WOMAN . . . . .Gina Gershon
MAN . . . . .Billy Strong

Lights up. A provocatively dressed woman sits on the bed. A man stands across the room, by the chair. He wears a suit.

WOMAN: So, how do you like it? Sitting, standing, or are you a traditional kind of guy?

MAN: What?

WOMAN: Tell you what; we'll improvise. *(She stands and crosses to him.)* Just see what happens, huh?

(She reaches for his jacket, as if to take it off him. He backs away from her.)

MAN: Don't do that.

WOMAN: Oh. Sorry. Some guys . . .

MAN: I don't want you to do that.

WOMAN: Whatever. *(She turns and takes off her skirt. Underneath she wears black stockings and panties.)* No shit, most guys like, you know, to be undressed. I think it reminds them of their mother, although I don't know why you'd want to be thinking about your mother at a time like this. I mean, I know about the whole psychology thing, Oedipus, what-ever — we do, we talk about that stuff — but I have to say I never believed most of it. That guys want to fuck their mothers. That just, frankly, that makes no sense to me. I mean, if it's true, you guys are even crazier than I thought, you know what I mean? I mean, no offense or anything.

MAN: Stop talking.

WOMAN: *(Unbuttoning her blouse.)* Oh, sorry. I know, I kind of run on. Especially late in the day; I get tired and anything that comes into my head comes right out of my mouth. I don't know. A lot of guys like it, which is lucky for me because I just, I don't even really know when it's happening —

MAN: Don't do that.

WOMAN: Excuse me?

MAN: Don't take your shirt off.

WOMAN: Oh. OK. *(She starts to button up again.)*

MAN: No. Leave it like that. I want to see that I can't see.

WOMAN: What?

MAN: If you button it, I can't see. I want to see that I can't see.

WOMAN: Oh. Sure.

(She stands for a moment, in the unbuttoned shirt and stockings. He stares at her. He is fully dressed.)

WOMAN: So . . . are we ready to get going here? I mean, I don't mean to rush things, but it's been my experience that it kind of helps to hit the ground running, you know, just let her rip, and since you're not particularly interested in small talk, we probably should just get to it, huh? *(Pause.)* So are we, what? You need a hand with this clothes thing here?

MAN: No.

WOMAN: No.

(Pause. They stare at each other.)

WOMAN: OK, sure, you're shy. I'm sensitive to that. We'll just take this real slow. *(She reaches for his jacket carefully.)*

MAN: Don't touch me.

WOMAN: Honey, that's not going to be entirely possible under the circumstances here —

(She tries to take the jacket off him. He shoves her, hard.)

WOMAN: Hey, don't get rough with me, asshole. That's not the deal, all right?

MAN: I told you. I don't want you to touch me. We don't do that.

WOMAN: Well, what do we do?

(He looks at her. He pulls the chair over, back to the audience. He sits in it.)

MAN: Stand here.

(He points in front of him. She crosses warily and faces him. His back is to the audience.)

WOMAN: *(Irritated.)* So, what, you just want to look, is that it? Fine. Whatever. But it's the same price, OK? We're not sailing into discount land because you're in some sort of fucking mood here, OK?

MAN: Don't say that.

WOMAN: I'm just telling you the rules.

MAN: No, I tell you the rules.

WOMAN: Listen —

MAN: I don't want you to use that word. You've used it twice. I don't want to hear that word.

WOMAN: What word?

MAN: You know the word.

WOMAN: What word? You mean fuck?

MAN: I don't want to hear it.

WOMAN: Sorry. I mean, I just, I thought that's what we were here for.

MAN: I DON'T WANT TO HEAR IT.

WOMAN: OK, fine, I won't say anything. I'll just stand here. You can pay me to stand here; that's fine by me. Fucking weirdo. Sorry.

(He sits, staring. Pause.)

MAN: Tell me what you want.

WOMAN: Tell you what I — you want me to tell you what I want?

MAN: Yes.

WOMAN: OK. I want to wrap this up and go home and see my kid. It's been a long day —

MAN: No.

WOMAN: No.

MAN: No.

WOMAN: That's not what I want.

MAN: No.

WOMAN: OK, then you tell me what I do want because I mean, I am in the dark here, all right? Usually, I have to say, usually there is not a lot of confusion about how to proceed, but —

MAN: Stop talking.

WOMAN: Stop talking. Right. I forgot.

MAN: Tell me what you want.

(Pause. She looks at him.)

WOMAN: *(Matter-of-fact.)* OK. Let's try this. I want you.

MAN: Yes.

WOMAN: Yes. That's a yes. Here we go. I want you . . . inside of me.

MAN: Yes.

WOMAN: Two yesses. This is a trend. I want to suck your cock.

MAN: No.

WOMAN: No. That's not what I want. OK, fine, I — fuck, I don't know what the fuck —

MAN: NO.

WOMAN: No, sorry, I didn't mean to use that word, I meant, I mean, I meant DARN. Darn.

MAN: Yes.

WOMAN: Yes. Darn. Sorry. I'm a little slow, darn it. *(Pause.)* I want you . . . in my mouth?

(He does not respond.)

WOMAN: I want . . . to touch you.

MAN: *(Quiet.)* No.

WOMAN: But I can't.

MAN: Yes.

WOMAN: I want you to look at me . . . and not see me.

MAN: Yes.

WOMAN: Yes. I want to stand in front of you naked, with clothes on.

MAN: Yes.

WOMAN: I get this. You want to have sex without sex.

MAN: *(Aroused.)* Yes. Tell me what you want.

> *(Pause. The Woman stares at him for a long moment, then turns and picks up her shoes.)*

WOMAN: No. I won't do it. This is sick, this is really —

MAN: Do you want the money or not?

> *(Pause.)*

WOMAN: Yeah. I want the money.

MAN: Then tell me what you want.

> *(Pause. The woman sets her shoes down, turns and looks at him.)*

WOMAN: I want . . . I want you in me outside of me.

MAN: Yes.

WOMAN: I want you to touch me . . . without feeling me. I want words with no voice. Sex with no heart. Love without bones.

MAN: *(Overlap.)* Yes. Yes.

WOMAN: *(Overlap.)* Skin without skin. I want blind eyes.

MAN: Yes.

WOMAN: I want you to stare me dead. I want you to lick me dry. I want you to take my words. Wipe me clean. Make me nothing. Let me be nothing for you. Let me be nothing. Let me be nothing.

MAN: *(Overlap.)* Yes. Yes. Yes!

> *(He comes without touching himself. She watches him, dispassionate. There is a long pause. They stare at each other.)*

MAN: You disgust me.

WOMAN: Yeah. I know. That'll be $200. Sir.

> *(Blackout.)*

END OF PLAY

GREAT TO SEE YOU

CHARACTERS

JILL
LIZA
RUDY

SET

A restaurant table

ORIGINAL PRODUCTION

Great to See You was originally produced at Naked Angels West in the summer of 1998, Mary-Pat Green, director, with the following cast:

JILL . . . . .Rebecca O'Brien
LIZA . . . . .Julie White
RUDY . . . . .Tim Ransom

A woman, Liza, sits alone. A man and a woman, Rudy and Jill, stand before her.

JILL: *(Excited.)* Hi —

LIZA: Oh —

JILL: It's so great to see you! You look exactly the same!

LIZA: So do you.

JILL: Oh, no —

RUDY: Hi.

(They sit.)

LIZA: Wow, it's great to see you.

RUDY: Yes.

LIZA: I wasn't sure, Rudy said you'd probably have to work —

JILL: When I heard you were in town, I got someone to take my shift! I mean it's been, God —

LIZA: A while.

JILL: Years, right?

LIZA: Something.

JILL: And what are you here for?

LIZA: Well, my parents live here.

JILL: Oh that's right. So vacation!

LIZA: A visit.

JILL: Well, it's just great that you could make time for us. I mean, I know you have to rush in and out of town.

LIZA: Of course I wanted to see you. It's been so long. *(There is an awkward pause.)* So how are your kids?

JILL: Just great. Benny's in preschool now, he's just a holy terror. And Doug's in second grade.

LIZA: Really? I mean, I can't — that's so big.

JILL: They love it here. Really love it. I'm so glad we moved back.

LIZA: It's a great town.

JILL: Heartland. If you're gonna raise kids, what else can you do?

LIZA: Well.

RUDY: How's your little girl?

LIZA: Great. She's great. Little. I mean, littler than — anyway. She's with her dad in England right now.

JILL: Oh that's right, your husband's British!

LIZA: Well, we're not — we never actually got — anyway.

JILL: Oh. You didn't —

LIZA: We're together. I mean, we're fine, everything's, we just never actually — I have a thing about the church, as you'll recall.

RUDY: *(A slight smile.)* Yes.

JILL: You didn't even want to —

LIZA: Actually, I have a thing about the government, too. Institutions in general.

JILL: Aren't you worried, about how it might . . . well, legally it does limit your rights. And internationally, I mean, if you got married you'd be able to work in England, wouldn't you?

LIZA: I can pretty much do that. I mean — you know, my work takes me there, a lot, and anyway, that wouldn't be why we did it. So I could work. *(Beat.)* It's hard to explain.

JILL: No! We completely understand.

(Pause.)

RUDY: So how is your work?

LIZA: Good. You know, very, it's a trip.

RUDY: You still with Sotheby's?

LIZA: Yeah. I worked the Jackie Kennedy auction, that was, good lord.

JILL: Oh, it must've been thrilling.

LIZA: Oh yeah. You know, touching history, that whole thing. And the people.

JILL: It must've been, just — great.

LIZA: It was kind of surreal actually. Of course the whole New York glitterati thing was going, like every celebrity in the city was there, even the ones who are above that sort of thing, and then they're all rubbing elbows with every rich conspiracy freak in the nation, I mean literally every nut job with cash pulled favors and got themselves in there, so it was a *scene.*

JILL: Well. Your life is a lot more exciting than ours.

LIZA: Oh, no, that's — no.

RUDY: Are you still painting?

LIZA: *(Beat.)* No.

JILL: Well, Rudy's going back to writing, did he tell you?

LIZA: *(Interested in this.)* No, that's great. I mean, I know you've —

RUDY: No —

JILL: Yes, he took the tests and everything! I tell all my friends my husband the doctor wants to quit his practice and become a novelist. They think it's a scream, but I think he should do it, don't you? I mean, it worked for Michael Crighton, didn't it? *(Checking her watch, reaching for her purse.)* Oh shoot, I have to call the sitter. The boys are at her house this week, because she has some sort of car thing, and I'm just not — here it is.

(She finds a piece of paper in her purse, and goes. There is an awkward pause.)

LIZA: I'm glad she came. I wasn't sure she could.

RUDY: No, she took off.

LIZA: That was nice of her.

RUDY: You look great. You look exactly the same.

(Liza nods, looks away, sad.)

LIZA: It's weird being back. I mean, good weird, sort of.

RUDY: I'd love to meet your little girl someday.

LIZA: Oh yeah. Next time. Usually, I bring her.

RUDY: You come often?

LIZA: No, not often. *(Beat, good-natured.)* So, you took some test to be a writer?

RUDY: *(Embarrassed.)* Oh —

LIZA: I didn't know there was a test. What is it, like, "draw this dog?"

RUDY: It wasn't anything. G.R.E.

LIZA: Oh, for graduate school?

RUDY: *(Embarrassed.)* It's not gonna happen. She loves it here, the boys love it here. It was a stupid idea.

LIZA: Can't you just write in your free time? *(Beat.)* What sort of thing do you want to write?

(Rudy shakes his head.)

LIZA: Are you all right?

RUDY: *(Too quick.)* Yes. I'm fine.

LIZA: You just seem —

RUDY: No. I'm fine. I don't seem anything.

LIZA: I'm sorry.

RUDY: Why? I mean, why are you sorry?

LIZA: Well, you seem — never mind. Oh, man. Maybe this wasn't such a good idea.

RUDY: No. Maybe it wasn't. I mean — Why are you here, anyway?

LIZA: *(Now irritated.)* Why am I here? I'm here because you — oh, man.

RUDY: What? I what?

LIZA: You didn't — that letter wasn't —

RUDY: It was just a card.

LIZA: It wasn't just a card, Rudy, it was very — between the lines, you were so —

RUDY: I wasn't anything between the lines. You don't know me anymore. I'm sorry, but you don't. You show up here, acting like — we haven't spoken in years, for God's sake. Years. You don't have the right to act like you know me.

LIZA: Yeah, well, you don't have the right to send me cards that say "I think of you every day."

(Jill returns.)

JILL: The machine was on. Can you believe that?

RUDY: Was it?

JILL: I mean, I like this babysitter, don't get me wrong, but it is unusual, bringing the boys to her house, and then for her to have the machine on. I suppose they could have gone to the library, but her car is not working, as we know, so that is just not very likely.

RUDY: Do you want to go over there?

JILL: No no. I'm just a little concerned is all.

LIZA: I understand, if you need to go.

JILL: No no no. I'm fine! And I never get to see you!

LIZA: I meant both of you could go. All of us. Maybe this just isn't a good time.

(Jill is surprised at this, and considering it.)

JILL: Oh. Well. Maybe we should, honey.

RUDY: *(Beat.)* If something were wrong, she'd call us. She has the number here, and the cell phone, and the beeper.

JILL: Absolutely.

RUDY: Yes.

(There is another unfortunate pause.)

LIZA: *(Trying.)* So, you guys bought a house?

JILL: It's great. So beautiful, you wouldn't even believe it. One of those Victorian painted ladies, well it's not painted, but it's in that school.

LIZA: And you probably paid like three cents for it, right? Everything's so affordable here, I can hardly stand it. Our place in Brooklyn, it's like two floors of a brownstone, a million five. Ridiculous.

JILL: A million?

LIZA: *(Now embarrassed.)* A million five.

JILL: Well. You must be doing very well. Of course, Sotheby's.

LIZA: Well, Michael does — he's in international real estate, and that's pretty much taken off. People buying things in other countries, it really rocks and rolls, over there in that market.

JILL: *(A little joke.)* And you haven't married this man?

LIZA: *(Beat.)* No. We're not married. *(Beat.)* We do have a kid, though, which always seems, to me, like the bigger commitment, actually.

JILL: Oh absolutely. Absolutely. Rudy and I just had our tenth anniversary.

LIZA: Ten? Really?

RUDY: Yes.

LIZA: Congratulations. I, you know, I didn't know it had been that long.

JILL: Oh yes. It was so romantic. I stole him away, he was completely surprised, but I arranged for us to spend the weekend in this lovely little B and B across the river.

LIZA: Sounds great.

RUDY: It was.

JILL: He didn't even know where we were going. I picked him up at the clinic and just said, we're not going home — his sister was staying with the boys — and I had everything we needed in the car. I had this beautiful basket of fruit and wine and cheese, and then I had bought this, you know, a peignoir, completely see through, it was gorgeous, all black lace, I had to work out for weeks just to feel good about wearing it. So we get to this place, this B and B, and I didn't know it when I booked the room, but it's run by these Baptists, I kid you not, and there's a sign right at the front, where you sign in, no alcohol. Can you imagine? No alcohol. So I think well, it's our anniversary, they can't keep us from just having a glass of wine, besides, there was something just kind of decadent about sneaking a bottle into our room so that's what we did. So then we get to our room, which is just so beautiful and quaint and private, and I made Rudy go into the bathroom so I can set everything up, and I open the wine, and lay out the fruit and I put on the peignoir, and I get on the bed, and I say you can come out now! And I start jumping on the bed. I don't know why I did it, but I just felt like it. *(She is laughing now.)* So there I am, jumping on the bed, completely naked under this beautiful peignoir, and he comes out and I jumped right on him and knocked him over, and he got this terrible gash in his head, from the table by the side of the bed, and he's bleeding all over and I've twisted my ankle, and then all those Baptists are knocking on the door, saying is everything all right in there? And there's that bottle of wine, and I'm stark naked on the floor, and Rudy's bleeding — it was a riot, just a riot.

(She smiles at Liza, who seems more or less stunned by this story.)

LIZA: Wow.

JILL: Oh, it was great. We laughed all night. After things calmed down.

LIZA: Yeah, had I known what fun marriage could be, maybe I would have tried it by now.

JILL: You should. You really should. We're so happy.

RUDY: Shouldn't we have seen a waiter by now?

JILL: You know you're right. *(Waving.)* Excuse me?

RUDY: Honey. Why don't you go ask? You need to check on the boys anyway.

JILL: I won't be a minute.

(She heads off. Liza looks down, then.)

LIZA: I have to go.

RUDY: Don't be ridiculous.

LIZA: God, could you not —

RUDY: If you left now, she'd know something was wrong.

LIZA: Rudy, she won't know anything. She lives completely on her own planet, as far as —

RUDY: Don't —

LIZA: No, don't you — you did what you had to do. I don't know why. You never bothered to tell me.

RUDY: That woman is my wife.

LIZA: OK, she's your wife, and you sit there like a demented brooding lump of clay whenever she's around, and send sad evasive touching cards to your ex-girlfriend behind her back! Yeah, you guys make marriage look great.

RUDY: That is not what is happening here.

LIZA: Yeah, OK Rudy.

(She stands and starts to go. He reaches over and grabs her arm to stop her. She stops. He continues to hold her arm.)

LIZA: Rudy. Let go of my arm.

RUDY: You are not leaving.

LIZA: Rudy, let go. You're right, we don't know each other anymore. This is stupid. I have a lot to do this afternoon, I'm only in town for the day anyway. Christ, it was ten years ago, who cares, now, who cares? *(Beat.)* Although why you had to go and get married to —

RUDY: You left.

LIZA: We were breaking up every other day, back then, it was ridiculous, we were making each other miserable. We're making each other miserable now! I have a kid. And you still probably go to church. Don't you. Don't you?

RUDY: Yes.

LIZA: Well.

(He kisses her hand.)

LIZA: Rudy, stop it, we're in public and your wife is around the corner and I refuse to be part of some tawdry scene.

(Jill reappears just as Liza breaks away and sits back down.)

JILL: Caught you!

(Oblivious, she laughs. Liza is distracted, Rudy sullen.)

JILL: Well, I was a complete failure. Couldn't find a waiter and left the phone number for the sitter in my purse. So I'm wandering out there like a fool and missing our whole visit! I'm sure someone will help us any minute.

LIZA: I don't know about that. Something's clearly gone wrong. Hasn't it? I mean, clearly, they've forgotten we're back here.

RUDY: I think they're a little shorthanded today.

LIZA: This never happens in New York, or London. I mean, those places are constantly packed but you get service right away.

JILL: *(A little testy.)* They're probably more used to it. Lots of people coming and going. It's just a little slower paced here, that's what we love about living here.

LIZA: Absolutely. *(Looking about.)* Who recommended this? Jill, you were the one who likes this place?

RUDY: *(Edgy.)* I do.

LIZA: Oh. 'Cause when I spoke with Jill, she said she picked the restaurant.

RUDY: She picked this one because I like it.

LIZA: I'm sure the food is great.

JILL: Well the atmosphere is really —

LIZA: Absolutely. Such a lovely corner. Lovely private corner. The atmosphere's fantastic, that's why they can't find us. We're not here to eat anyway; we're here to *visit.* *(She slaps the table for emphasis.)* You guys look great. Time is serving us all so well.

JILL: Did Rudy tell you, we're thinking of having another baby?

LIZA: *(A beat.)* No. He didn't mention it.

JILL: Well, by adoption. That's what we're thinking. I just desperately want a girl, and the only way to guarantee that is to get one already cooked, so to speak! I know it takes forever, even for people like us, a stable family et cetera et cetera so we are looking into foreign adoption, which makes me a little nervous, because of all the reports about how disturbed and sick those children are, but I think if we keep our focus on maybe South America. Some cute little Guatemalan baby, something like that. Of course for some reason most of them are boys so maybe it really is my fate to just be surrounded by boys!

LIZA: *(At her wit's end.)* If you want a girl, why don't you go to China?

JILL: We thought of that. I just think that culturally it's too far.

LIZA: Further than Guatemala?

JILL: Oh yes.

LIZA: Wow. OK. I uh, actually, never thought of it that way.

RUDY: We're very excited.

JILL: Oh, just thrilled.

LIZA: *(Distracted and mean.)* You don't know your sitter's phone number by heart?

JILL: Excuse me?

LIZA: Before, when you tried to call, you left the number here.

JILL: Oh. You know, you're right, but she's got one of those numbers it's just impossible to remember! There's not like two fours or three ones, nothing, every number is different and none of them are sequential — you know, six seven eight or two three four. That's why. And I have the number right on my refrigerator door, so if she doesn't show up, I know right where to go.

LIZA: What if you're at work, what about that?

JILL: If I'm at work, she's at my house. Besides, I carry it with me, that's what I do. I carry it with me. Here it is.

LIZA: Oh you're right. There it is. So you could call.

JILL: I think they're fine.

LIZA: Well, if you're comfortable, sure. I just thought, since before you didn't get through.

RUDY: They're fine.

LIZA: It's me. I just wouldn't be comfortable.

JILL: *(Conceding.)* You're right.

RUDY: No, they're fine.

JILL: It'll just make me feel a little better. I'll be right back.
    (She goes. Liza calls after her.)

LIZA: And check on the waiter while you're at it!

RUDY: *(As soon as Jill's gone.)* Are you proud of yourself?

LIZA: *(Angry.)* I don't know. Are you?

RUDY: I have nothing to be ashamed of.

LIZA: That is what you married. That.

RUDY: How dare you.

LIZA: How dare *you?* Is that how you two talk to each other? Is that it? And you're gonna adopt a kid. Oh that's a good idea. You guys have the most dysfunctional relationship this side of my parents and —

RUDY: There is nothing —

LIZA: You're a genius and she's a dingdong!

RUDY: I am hardly a genius.

LIZA: Yeah you're right. I gotta qualify what I used to think about you, having met your —

RUDY: Do not —

LIZA: I'd like to kill you. *(There is a tense pause.)* You slept with her, didn't you?

Before you got married. She was the one. You didn't get her pregnant, you just slept with her because all that Catholic shit inside you was finally making you a little too nuts, so one night you lost it and you slept with whoever was around, and it was her, and then you had to marry her. That's what happened. You couldn't sleep with me, even though you loved me, you had to sleep with whoever, and then —

RUDY: I love her.

LIZA: You loved *me*. And with all due respect, I don't believe that one person could love both of us, Rudy.

RUDY: Shut up.

LIZA: You stop sending me letters!

(She stands to go. He stands to stop her. She leans over and kisses him. In no time flat they are making out passionately. It goes on for quite a long time, and goes really too far. Occasionally one of them looks up and around, vaguely worried that someone — say, Jill — is going to see them, but their concern is generally much too fleeting. The table settings go flying. Finally, they stop, breathless, and silently part. Liza goes back to her side of the table. They both sit, silent, not looking at each other for a long moment. Liza makes a halfhearted attempt to straighten out the tablecloth. Jill returns and sits.)

JILL: *(Oblivious.)* Well, I spoke to the maitre'd. Apparently one of his waiters didn't show up today but he said he would get right on it. Has anyone been over here? What happened to the table? Well, now this is really ridiculous. *(Waving off.)* But I did get hold of the babysitter. They were out back on her swing set. I just don't understand why she couldn't take a phone with her, that's all. Really, this is — well, the table is a mess! *(She briefly looks back and forth between them, not comprehending what's going on.)* Well, I hope you two got through all your reminiscing while I was gone because I am not leaving this table again.

LIZA: Yes. We got through it.

JILL: Good! It's so good to see old friends. Really, you look great. *(Taking Rudy's hand.)* Doesn't she look great? *(Looking off.)* And here comes the waiter! Now everything's in place, and we can just have a lovely meal. *(Happy, she waves to the approaching waiter. Blackout.)*

END OF PLAY

THE ACTRESS

CHARACTERS
MIKE

NINA

SET
A beach

ORIGINAL PRODUCTION
The Actress was originally produced at HB Studio in June 2002, Nina Steiger, director, with the following cast:

MIKE . . . . .Peter Appel

NINA . . . . .Fiona Gallagher

Mike and Nina walking on a beach. Mike carries a lot of stuff. Nina is looking for a good spot.

NINA: This looks great. Right here. Is this great or what?
   (Mike sets the stuff down. Nina moves five feet to the left.)
NINA: *(Continuing.)* Wait a minute. This is . . . no wait. *(Moving to the right again.)* No wait. Right here. No wait.
MIKE: Nina!
NINA: Right here, that's what I'm saying, right here.
   (She starts to take her wrap off, five feet from where Mike is. Resigned, he picks up all the stuff again and moves to the spot she's picked.)
NINA: *(Continuing.)* This is incredible. The ocean? I mean, it's incredible, right?
   (Without waiting for a reply to anything, she just continues to talk, while Mike unloads.)
   Oh, you were so right. This was just what I needed, just a break from everything. Four days at the beach, it's just brilliant, you know, absolutely, the sound of the waves, I mean, that is a meditation all it's own. A meditation. Sun. Water. Birds. You'd have to be nuts not to see the beauty in this. It's so relaxing.
MIKE: I told you.
NINA: That's what I'm saying, you told me and you were right, I said you were so so right. *(She slathers suntan lotion on herself, talking.)* I mean, I did not want to do that stupid workshop. That play just sucked, yet another opportunity to play some idiot doing things that make no fucking sense whatsoever, for no money, that no one is ever going to produce. I mean, someone should put these poor playwrights out of their misery. Who fucking needs it.
MIKE: This is better.
NINA: Please! Are you kidding? Look at this! I so needed this. After that pilot season, oh my God, you know they keep saying this is the worst one yet and then the next one is just worst. It's like how do they keep getting worse? But they do! It's so fucking demoralizing.
MIKE: Nobody got anything.
NINA: Nobody got anything! Who are they hiring anymore? It's like they go out and look and look and look until they find the worst actors out there and then they're the ones they give all the jobs too!
MIKE: It sucks.
NINA: It so totally sucks.

MIKE: This is better.

NINA: This is so totally better, are you kidding? Because I am just completely disgusted with it. I mean, I didn't even get close this year. Last year at least I got close, that cops and public defenders in Manhattan show, I almost had that, but no they had to hire a movie star . . . oh shoot. Why am I thinking about that again? Six callbacks. I thought I was going to have heart failure.

MIKE: They do that to everybody.

NINA: *(Suddenly vulnerable.)* No, I know, I just . . . you know how when something that disappointed you just comes up again, all of a sudden? Oh, shoot. On such a pretty day? Why does that happen? I thought I was over that. *(Beat, sad.)* I really wanted that. I would have been good in that.

MIKE: It didn't make it on the air anyway.

NINA: *(Putting the lid back on it.)* Thank God, that script was just the stupidest thing I ever read in my life. And that cow they hired, please God help me, she can't act her way out of a paper bag, that's why her movie career dried up! I mean, does it make sense to hire someone who is a total fucking failure as an actress, just because she was bad in a couple of movies in her twenties?

MIKE: You want to take a walk?

NINA: No, I'm relaxing, this is so relaxing, just being here. Don't you think this is relaxing?

MIKE: Yeah. No, yeah.

NINA: I am so relaxed. Those fuckers. Those fuckheads. Who fucking needs it. I am a fucking artist, I do not fucking need this kind of fucking rejection every day.

MIKE: Nobody does.

NINA: I know. Fuckers. This is so relaxing.

(She leans back in her chair, looks at the sky. Mike listens to the roar of the waves. Nina shifts in her seat.)

NINA: *(Continuing.)* And I was not going to do that workshop anyway. That play is idiotic.

MIKE: Nina.

NINA: I mean, how many fucking bad plays can you do before you just get completely fucking demoralized?

MIKE: I know but you know. I mean. You know?

NINA: Because fuck.

MIKE: You want a soda or something?

NINA: I would love a soda.

MIKE: Here.

(He gets a soda for her out of the cooler, gets one for himself. She opens it, takes a drink, looks around. He does the same.)

MIKE: (*Continuing.*) God, that tastes great. You know, that is a damn good fucking can of soda. Sodas on the beach. Sometimes I am really just grateful. Because this is . . . I mean, life is . . . I mean, look at that stupid bird. That is so beautiful. Look at him, just . . .

NINA: Oh yeah.

MIKE: Right?

NINA: Fuck yes. This was a fantastic idea, coming out here. As opposed to what, hanging around the city and doing some loser workshop of a bad play, this is a no fucking brainer.

(Mike nods, not knowing how to respond.)

MIKE: This is a good soda.

NINA: I mean, I'm an actress. You know? I am an interpretive fucking artist. Give me something to interpret, why don't you, then you'll see something. All I ever do is audition for shit, total shit, that's all anyone is doing anymore. Television, film, the theater, all of it, it's completely unwatchable.

MIKE: Maybe you should take some time off. I mean, maybe that would actually be good for you.

NINA: What is that supposed to mean?

MIKE: I mean . . .

NINA: You mean stop?

MIKE: No no, that's not what I mean. I just mean, I don't do it anymore and it's fine.

NINA: What do you mean, you don't do it?

MIKE: Come on, Nina, I don't — I mean, I don't do it. I haven't been on an audition in five months.

NINA: It was a shitty pilot season, everyone knows that.

MIKE: That's not what I mean.

NINA: No one got anything.

MIKE: Listen, I don't feel bad about it. You don't have to make me feel better.

NINA: I'm not.

MIKE: It's just, I don't know. I think I decided that I like being a bartender. The people come in and talk to you, it's interesting. They all do so many different things, and you know, you're a bartender so they want to talk to you. And I realized that every time somebody told me what they did,

I'm a lawyer, I'm a real estate broker, I work in a shoe store, I'd say, yea, I'm an actor. Like I wanted to let them know that I wasn't really a bartender, I was really not what it looked like I was. And everybody was always really nice about it. But it just hit me one day, that I was being kind of dumb. To be spending your life thinking that what you were doing wasn't real, like you're just doing that while you're waiting to do something else with the rest of your life? So for a couple days, I did this experiment, whenever people told me what they did, I said, I'm a bartender. That's what I told them. I'm a bartender. And it felt kind of good, you know. It actually did. I like being a bartender. I like not thinking about what I'm not all the time.

NINA: Everybody needs to take time off once in a while.

MIKE: I'm not taking time off. I'm a bartender. I'm a bartender, sitting on a beach.

NINA: Well, I don't know how to respond to that.

MIKE: You don't have to respond.

NINA: So, what, you want me to say, I'm a caterer sitting on the beach?

MIKE: That's not what I'm saying.

NINA: No fucking way. I think I'm a little better than that. If you don't mind.

MIKE: That's not what I'm saying.

NINA: I don't know what you're saying.

(A beat.)

MIKE: It's just, I thought it would be good to get away.

NINA: I said it was, what have I been saying?

MIKE: I know you have, I just . . .

NINA: I should have done that workshop.

MIKE: No, come on.

NINA: There were a lot of people coming to see that. After the shitty pilot season I just had, I cannot afford to just turn down work.

MIKE: Come on, Nina. That's not what I meant, at all.

NINA: Well, what did you mean? You meant I should just admit I'm not an actress —

MIKE: No —

NINA: I should just give up my entire identity —

MIKE: No, come on —

NINA: Well, I'm just not ready to do that all right? I still have a dream of being an artist. I'm not going to apologize for that and I'm not going to just give it up. It's the best part of me. I can't just give that up.

(Beat.)

MIKE: Don't do it. Come on.

NINA: I'm sorry if you don't understand that.

MIKE: I do understand that, Nina —

NINA: I am not giving up everything I have worked, you know how hard I work —

MIKE: Yeah but, that's what I'm saying. We can —

NINA: Maybe it never meant the same thing to you.

MIKE: OK maybe it didn't but you do. You do, and and a baby —

NINA: I just can't be asked —

MIKE: Come on, honey. Come on. I think we should have it —

NINA: Do you know what it does to your figure? It's hard enough to get work. It's hard enough.

MIKE: I can take care of us. I love you. Come on. I love you.

NINA: That's not the point.

(Beat.)

Is this why you asked me to do this? A couple of days away at the beach so you could, you could hound me about this?

MIKE: *(Beat.)* I just thought it would be good to get away.

NINA: *(Beat.)* I should have done that workshop.

(She cannot look at him. Blackout.)

END OF PLAY

FUNERAL PLAY

CHARACTERS

ORIGINAL PRODUCTION

Funeral Play was originally produced at HB Studio in June 2001, Max Mayer, director, with the following cast:

Roy is sitting alone next to the coffin, grieving quietly. Jim enters, cautious. He considers him for a long moment, not sure about interrupting. Finally, he clears his throat. Roy looks up, startled.

JIM: Hi. Hello. *(Beat.)* I'm sorry for your loss.
(Roy nods, goes back to his meditation. Jim tries to think about how to begin again.)

JIM: *(Continuing.)* When is the service? This afternoon? The service is this afternoon?

ROY: People will be, visiting, in, half an hour. I was hoping to just have a few minutes alone with her before people started to arrive.
(Having gently made his suggestion, Roy tries to meditate some more. Jim shifts on his feet, awkward.)

JIM: Oh of course. Absolutely. *(Checking the coffin.)* Your mother, huh? I mean, you've, uh, lost your mother, I guess.

ROY: Yes.

JIM: That's a hard thing. To lose a parent. To lose your mother. Unless you weren't close. Of course sometimes that makes it worse. I mean some people I think feel OK about it but that's not normal or healthy or . . . sorry. *(Beat.)* You don't remember me, do you?

ROY: No.

JIM: That's OK. I mean, I don't blame you, you're going through a very hard, very stressful, I mean — well, how could you remember someone you met sort of in passing, not passing exactly but . . . anyway.

ROY: Listen. I don't mean to be rude.

JIM: You really don't remember? The Imperial Rest versus the Eternal Slumber? The Nocturnal Peace?

ROY: *(Recognizing him.)* Oh.

JIM: Yeah.

ROY: Roy. *(At a loss.)* Yes. Well . . . How are you?

JIM: OK. So it worked out? The . . .
(He points to the coffin.)

ROY: Yes. Thank you.
(He touches the coffin, reverent.)

JIM: Good, good. That's what I . . . I just wanted to make sure. *(Beat.)* Because there was a little confusion, actually. Downstairs. When they were, actually I'm not even sure where the confusion, but you know, there was so much you had to deal with, I'm sure, the flowers and the guest list, open or shut, which, you know, which coffin. A lot of questions during what is unquestionably a very, very sad time.

ROY: Look, is there something you . . . need?

JIM: No no. I just, because of the confusion. There are a lot of funerals that happen right on top of each other, back to back, well, that's not the right, anyway, people die, and everyone, sometimes many funerals happen at the same time, and there are several bodies to be prepared, downstairs, and the coffins line up, they, there are often several, in a row, downstairs. I'm sure you can imagine how that would happen.

(Roy looks in the coffin, worried, then looks at Jim.)

ROY: *(Defensive.)* That is my mother.

JIM: Yes. Yes, oh, I didn't mean to imply otherwise. It is. It's just not . . . her coffin.

(Roy looks at him, uncomprehending.)

JIM: (*Continuing.*) You know, we had the conversation? Imperial Rest, with the satin lining and the brass fixtures, not to mention the goose down, that's, it runs several thousand more than the Eternal Slumber, not to mention the more, um, economical but perfectly, perfectly reasonable, fine, Nocturnal — you know, the Nocturnal —

ROY: Peace.

JIM: Exactly so.

(There is a pause. Jim is very unhappy. Roy looks at the coffin.)

ROY: We're very happy with our selection, is that what you're asking?

JIM: Yes, I guess so. *(Beat.)* Because it's not actually, you see, your selection. You paid for, that is, you selected the Nocturnal Peace, and somehow, well, frankly, through my — confusion — or, some might say, error — your mother was placed in the Imperial Rest, which was actually paid for by Mr. and Mrs. James Riordan, of Canarsie, for her grandmother may she rest, you know, in et cetera.

(He is silent. Roy considers this.)

ROY: So this isn't my, my mother's coffin, that's what you're saying.

JIM: Unfortunately no.

ROY: So what are you, what are we supposed to — people are coming. People are arriving, my father and his — all their friends not to mention my siblings and — people are coming to mourn, to mourn her.

JIM: Absolutely, absolutely.

ROY: I mean what are you saying, that we're expected — because of your screwup, this is a terrible thing for our family. She was a deeply loved woman, we all are in real —

JIM: I hear you —

ROY: And you want what? What is it you want, for us to move her body into a different coffin because of your mistake? I don't care about your mistakes now! My mother is dead, and the people who loved her are gathering, today, now, gathering to —

JIM: No no I totally —

ROY: This is not my problem! Now, would you please get out of here so I can spend a few — my mother is dead, you asshole.

JIM: I see. OK. You're completely right. I just wanted to mention it.

ROY: Well, you did. And I intend, this is completely unacceptable. At a time like this to be asked — I intend to let people know I find this completely unacceptable.

(He sits, puts his hand on the coffin, protective. Jim nods, miserable.)

JIM: Of course. I'm sorry. I didn't mean to disturb you.

ROY: Well, you did. You are! Why are you still here, will you just please leave me in peace, in some small amount of peace before I have to put my mother in the ground? What is — I am going to report you. I, understand me, I will have your job over this.

(Beat. Jim thinks about what to say to this. Roy sits, angry, by the coffin, waiting for him to leave.)

JIM: Well.

ROY: Well, what? Well why are you still here? How many times do I have to ask you to just get the hell out of here?

JIM: You know, you — I know you're upset, but you shouldn't be mean. I'm upset too, all right? I mean, there's no point in your threatening to, to have me fired. I've already been — it was on the outside chance, I mean, that I could maybe get my job back, that is why I came here, to see, to see if at this terrible time in your life you might have a little, maybe, compassion for a fellow traveler, that was the reason I thought to speak to you.

ROY: If you don't get out of here now, I will call your ex-boss and have you thrown out. Christ.

JIM: *(Angry.)* Listen — hey — listen — ask yourself, you just need to ask yourself then, if I came here and told you that you got a cheaper coffin, than than than the one you paid for, if you would think it was such a crazy idea, that you should switch the coffins. You ask yourself that. I mean, you act all outraged, but you wouldn't think it was so nuts if the whole money thing went in the other direction.

ROY: *(Enraged.)* What?

JIM: Yes, oh, you're all enraged but I'm right, aren't I, I saw the logic in your —
at time like this you would think of money, you and my sister, you're
exactly — I mean, I lost my job over this, I — and my mother's dead,
too, you know. She died, it wasn't that long ago, I feel your pain. My
mother died, I was the only one there, my stupid sister is in BALtimore,
and she can't be bothered, my father is at home in a wheelchair and I
can't call him, from the hospital and tell him, so much was happening
so fast, and besides which they didn't know, they didn't see it coming
although she did. She did, and I — so you can just — I mean, I know,
I know, so many things just happening at once, and the doctors, no one
will tell you — meanwhile, my sister the IDIOT cannot be reached, they
want to know about putting Mom on machines, which she did not
want, it was so clear, she signed a document, and when I call Dad he just
breaks down and wants to come down to the hospital but he's home
alone, and I can't, she's going, I wasn't, to leave her? How could I? Can
you tell me that? Because I was — to have to say good-bye so quickly —
I'm sorry, but — to have to say good-bye so quickly to someone — I
mean, I was there, and for that I am grateful, for all of it, the confusion,
and the horror, not being able to, to say what — I am grateful. To have
been there. And I did, I did close her eyes. Which was very hard, very
hard, but I wanted to do it for her. Because I loved her very much. And
then of course there was hell to pay, my father, why I didn't have them
turn those machines on so that he would have time to come down there,
his anger — which probably was just his grief redirected, although
frankly you do get tired of having every one of his vast array of emotions
redirected into anger so that he can dump it right on you — whatever.
Whatever. And then there's my sister, who breezes into town after all of
it and just takes over. Which coffin, what kind of flowers, what readings
at the service, Bach and Shubert for the processional, she's just on top of
everything and I am no longer, believe me, so the funeral is absolutely
perfect and there's nothing of my mother in it. Nothing at all. And
they're both so angry with me, for the way I — but I couldn't do it, I
just couldn't. Put her on those machines just for them. It would have
been wrong. And now of course they will both, yes, of course I have lost
another job, well, I don't know why I took it anyway, to take a job in a
funeral home three months after your mother dies, that's just crazy,
unless it's just so you can keep, keep . . . *(Beat.)* Sorry. Really, I'm sorry.
I just, uh, I do feel your pain, and I know you want to be with your

mother today. To have this time. I know that. I envy you that. *(Beat.)* I do, I envy you that.

(Beat.)

ROY: Look. Do you want to sit down?

JIM: No, no, I —

ROY: No, really. You need to take a few minutes.

JIM: I . . .

ROY: It's OK. Really. Go ahead. Here.

(He gestures toward his seat, next to the coffin.)

JIM: Oh.

ROY: Please. She would like that. She would.

(He gestures again. Jim goes to the seat, sits. Roy stands to one side of him. After a moment, Jim reaches out and touches the coffin. He takes a minute. Roy bows his head, steps over and touches the coffin as well. As the two men say good-bye to their mothers we:)

(Fade to black.)

END OF PLAY

TRAIN TO BROOKLYN

CHARACTERS

JULIA
STEPHANIE
HOLLY

ORIGINAL PRODUCTION

Train to Brooklyn was originally produced at HB Studio under the title *No Exit* in June 2003, Marcia Jean Kurtz, director, with the following cast:

JULIA . . . . .Kathryn Grody
STEPHANIE . . . . .Alexandra Napier
HOLLY . . . . .Carole Monferdini

Three women, Julia, Stephanie, and Holly, are sitting next to each other on a stopped train. They hold gaily-wrapped presents and are dressed in pretty party clothes. There is a long moment of silence.

JULIA: This is a nightmare.

STEPHANIE: It hasn't been that long. What did they say? It's a police action. They're probably just taking some drunk off the train in front of us, or something.

JULIA: Or, it's a terrorist attack.

STEPHANIE: That's not what it is.

HOLLY: I hope that's not what it is!

STEPHANIE: That's not what it is! If it were something serious, they'd tell us!

JULIA: You live in an extraordinary universe.

STEPHANIE: No, I don't.

(There is a moment of silence.)

JULIA: It's been at least fifteen minutes since the last announcement. Just since the last announcement.

STEPHANIE: No, it hasn't. They make those announcements every five minutes.

JULIA: They do not. Excuse me? Are you kidding?

STEPHANIE: What? They do, every five minutes —

JULIA: You mean, there's a rule, that they follow, the MTA has rules that you have to make an announcement every —

STEPHANIE: I think so, yes. I read that somewhere. In the *Times*, I think.

JULIA: *The New York Times* is reporting on how often they make announcements on the subway.

STEPHANIE: I think so. Yes. That's where I read it. They're very concerned about the MTA since all the budget crisis and that's where I read it.

JULIA: You live in an extraordinary universe.

STEPHANIE: I live in the same universe you live in.

JULIA: I don't think you do. Sorry, Holly. Sisters!

HOLLY: Oh, I know! Well, I don't know, I don't have a sister. But you know.

JULIA: You've known us both a long time.

HOLLY: Twenty years.

STEPHANIE: I'm sure we'll make it on time.

HOLLY: Oh, it's a baby shower. Nobody cares if you're a little late for a baby shower!

STEPHANIE: That's right. She's not going to care.

JULIA: She is absolutely going to care.

HOLLY: No — no —

JULIA: No, I mean, let's just not kid ourselves about that. Kate is not the kind of person who just doesn't care if people show up an hour late. She is not someone who things more or less roll off of. She's going to care.

STEPHANIE: Well, that's her problem then. We got on the subway in plenty of time.

JULIA: Yes, except we weren't supposed to be taking the subway.

STEPHANIE: I know, but —

JULIA: Because I would never have agreed, ahead of time, to take the subway. To Brooklyn? Are you crazy?

STEPHANIE: It doesn't take that long, usually.

JULIA: We've been on this train for an hour!

STEPHANIE: *(Defensive.)* It hasn't been an hour, actually, it's been forty minutes, and it's only been that long because there's a train stuck in the station ahead of us for a police action and that could happen anywhere. That happens EVERYWHERE in Manhattan. It has nothing to do with going to Brooklyn. It doesn't take that long to go to Brooklyn, it really doesn't, I do it all the time!

HOLLY: You do?

STEPHANIE: Yes, I have friends, I visit friends in Brooklyn. All the time. If you take the Battery Tunnel, it takes twenty minutes to get there.

JULIA: When you drive.

STEPHANIE: *(Knows she made a slip here.)* Yes. I mean — when I drive, I take the Battery Tunnel.

JULIA: But we're not driving today, are we?

STEPHANIE: Julia, look. I said I was sorry.

JULIA: It's just —

STEPHANIE: *(Snapping.)* I said I was sorry! I am sorry! I'm sorry! Brian needed the car!

JULIA: So did you.

STEPHANIE: Well, he needed it worse. He's got Noah this weekend, what was I supposed to say?

JULIA: You were supposed to say, I've promised Julia and Holly I would drive them to Kate's baby shower —

STEPHANIE: I mentioned that, I did —

JULIA: You "mentioned" it?

HOLLY: *(Mediating.)* It's OK —

STEPHANIE: *(Ignoring this.)* I told him. I was very firm.

JULIA: You weren't that firm —

STEPHANIE: I was. I was! He was taking Noah to a baseball game and he was very adamant, because of the political situation, about not wanting to take him on the subway! He's my son! What am I supposed to say to that!

JULIA: You're supposed to say you're being manipulative and shitty and no you can't have the car and parking out at either stadium is a complete nightmare, what are you insane, stop acting like you give a shit about my son, you've ignored both of us for years and I'm not falling for this bullshit, I'll see you in court.

STEPHANIE: That's very useful.

JULIA: He would understand it. He would understand what it really means, which is you are not pushing me around in court you son of a bitch.

HOLLY: Has he been horrible?

STEPHANIE: He's been difficult.

JULIA: He's been horrible. Horrible. And this is a complete excuse, you're never going to get that car back now. How much do you want to bet on it? That's the last you'll ever see of the Volvo.

STEPHANIE: He can't do that.

JULIA: Stephanie, I have told you for years —

STEPHANIE: I don't want to talk about it!

JULIA: That man has never been anything but manipulative and selfish and abusive to both you and Noah —

STEPHANIE: *(Upset now.)* I don't want to talk about it!

(There is another moment of silence. Holly shifts, uncomfortable.)

HOLLY: It's fun being in New York. I mean, this isn't, obviously, being stuck on a train underneath the East River isn't exactly "fun," but I don't know. I should try and get down more. I used to just like walking around the streets so much. It's so haunting. New York. The Flat Iron Building, I could just look at that forever. I mean, I love North Adams, the community is so sweet. But it's different.

STEPHANIE: *(Strained, but trying.)* How long have you been there, now?

HOLLY: Oh. Fifteen years! We didn't mean to stay that long, of course, but when Paul got tenure, it seemed like that was too good to pass up. It's a nice town. They love him, at the university. They really love him.

JULIA: *(A little too cool.)* How's your dissertation going?

(There is an awkward pause at this.)

HOLLY: Oh, not — I'm — the chapter I'm working on is, there's a lot of good . . .

JULIA: Uh huh.

HOLLY: Oh. Well. You're right, of course, I'll probably never finish it. I'm — just — ridiculous, aren't I? I'm . . . oh. What stop was it? Something with a B, I think.

(She stands and goes to look at the map. Stephanie turns and gives Julia a dirty look.)

JULIA: What?

STEPHANIE: "What."

JULIA: *(Insulted.)* Yes. What?

STEPHANIE: Nothing.

(Holly returns, trying more successfully to be bright now.)

HOLLY: Bergen Street. That must be it, it's the only B up there.

STEPHANIE: *(Kind, good-natured.)* Would you like a brownie, Holly?

HOLLY: You have brownies?

JULIA: I thought those were for the shower.

STEPHANIE: She won't miss two or three.

(She reaches into her bag and takes out a tin of brownies, which she proceeds to open.)

JULIA: Kate? Kate will absolutely miss two or three.

STEPHANIE: How will she know?

JULIA: Those are for the shower, Stephanie.

STEPHANIE: Who cares? Holly?

(She hands one to Holly.)

HOLLY: I really shouldn't. Sweets are so bad for you, I hardly ever eat them.

STEPHANIE: You're stuck on the subway. Live a little.

(She hands her a brownie.)

STEPHANIE: *(Continuing; cold.)* Julia. You want one?

JULIA: No. I'll wait.

STEPHANIE: Suit yourself.

HOLLY: *(Eating.)* Oh my God. This is incredible. What is in this?

STEPHANIE: Chocolate, chocolate chips, white chocolate chips, macadamia nuts, coconut, and caramel.

HOLLY: This is amazing.

STEPHANIE: *(Eating.)* Mmm. It's Noah's favorite.

HOLLY: This is so good. Where did you learn to do this?

STEPHANIE: I just made it up. We made it up together one day. You know, you're baking, and throwing things in there, and you ask him, should I put this in, or that in.

JULIA: And of course he told you to put everything in.

STEPHANIE: Yes, he did, and so I did. That's what I did. And I know you would never do that with your kids, Julia, and I appreciate that. I do! I just — God!

JULIA: What are you so upset about?

STEPHANIE: What am I — are you kidding? Are you kidding here? We've been stuck on the subway for how long, we're going to a baby shower for someone I don't much like, we're stuck, and you — I'm getting divorced! I feel shitty! I feel like a complete horrible failed person! OK? My son is with my husband God knows where, and you're being a complete, heaven forbid, I mean, you're my sister! You're my only sister and I'm in trouble here, and you're — Jesus! God! I'm getting divorced! I'm in trouble!

JULIA: It wasn't my idea to take the train. Just remember that. I thought we were driving. I said we should drive. I said, we should drive!

STEPHANIE: OK. You did. You really did.

(Beat.)

HOLLY: These are really good brownies.

(There is a sudden jolt, and the train starts to move.)

HOLLY: (*Continuing.*) Oh, look! The train is moving! See! We're not late! We're not going to be late at all! That is a stroke of luck! Really! Aren't we lucky. I mean — even though I have no children, and you're both miserable — we are all so lucky.

(She smiles down at her brownie, as the train starts to move. Fade to black.)

END OF PLAY

HOW WE GET TO WHERE WE'RE GOING

CHARACTERS
    BRIAN
    PETE

SET
    A bare office with a desk and two chairs

ORIGINAL PRODUCTION
    How We Get to Where We're Going was originally produced at The
    Culture Project in October 2004, Sherry Kaller, director, with the fol-
    lowing cast:

    BRIAN . . . . .Chris Messina
    PETE . . . . .Tim Ransom

Two men, Brian and Pete, spitballing on either side of a desk. They both wear suits, the jackets over the backs of their chairs. Brian holds a legal pad, and a pen. Occasionally, he reluctantly writes a few things down.

BRIAN: I don't —

PETE: Just hypothetically.

BRIAN: Hypothetically.

PETE: Yeah, hypothetically —

BRIAN: *(Overlap.)* Because even hypothetically it makes me, I don't, you know —

PETE: Oh for God's sake.

BRIAN: No, I mean even discussing a hypothetical what, what are we talking about, a hypothetical situation?

PETE: The situation is real. I mean, these people present a real threat —

BRIAN: How? How do they —

PETE: Oh, come on, Bri —

BRIAN: What? I'm serious —

PETE: I don't have to have this conversation.

BRIAN: You were the one —

PETE: How do they present a threat? Seventy percent, everyone in America is screaming about the reality of the threat. I don't have to defend —

BRIAN: Everyone in America does not —

PETE: *(With finality.)* — I don't have to defend my use of the word *threat.*

BRIAN: *(Not budging now.)* I just think that perhaps the word *threat* is being overused right now. All these alerts, we're always being threatened, orange alert, red alert, blue alert, it doesn't MEAN anything, to to to —

PETE: They're breaking the law. They're threatening the civic, civic balance —

BRIAN: There is no such thing as civic balance!

PETE: The fuck there isn't. A democracy is an organism. A fragile but vital living thing —

BRIAN: Oh, my —

PETE: You cannot, are you going to argue every point that comes out of my mouth?

BRIAN: I don't want to talk about democracy.

PETE: That's what we're talking about!

BRIAN: No. We're talking, hypothetically —

PETE: Look, we got to come up with something, or we're both out on our asses. You surely know that.

(Beat.)

BRIAN: Then this isn't hypothetical.

PETE: How do I know if it's hypothetical or not, you won't even let me talk about it!

(Beat.)

BRIAN: They're not going to fire you or me.

PETE: They're not going to fire *me*.

BRIAN: Oh, that's —

PETE: What?

BRIAN: That's, they're not, you know, this is the same thing that we're talking about, you say shit like that and then I'm supposed to be all, oh, am I going to lose my job if I don't, orange alert! Orange alert! We're at orange alert! *(Beat, Pete stares at him. Unnerved.)* That's bullshit.

PETE: This is a waste of time. I'm going home.

(He stands, grabs his jacket and shrugs it on. After a long moment, Brian speaks.)

BRIAN: OK. Did someone say something? I mean, why would you say something like that?

PETE: No one said anything.

BRIAN: That's what I mean.

PETE: You feel secure. Good.

BRIAN: No, I don't feel secure! Who the fuck feels secure anymore, I don't even — fuck. Fuck, man. Oh, fuck you. This is fucked.

PETE: They're not kidding around, Bri.

BRIAN: You are so —

PETE: I'm just saying, think outside the box. I think it's been made clear that that is our mandate under this administration. Is that not clear to you?

BRIAN: Think outside the box, I hate that. As soon as people started saying "think outside the box," the fact that everyone was saying it meant that thinking outside the box was already completely inside the box. So it always, from the START it meant the OPPOSITE of what it pretended to mean, and anyway, what box? What box are we even talking about? Like "pushing the envelope," what was that supposed to ever mean, huh? "Pushing the envelope," was that supposed to mean that we were pushing envelopes off the table, and why, by the way, were we metaphorically supposed to be doing that? "Pushing the envelope," it didn't ever MEAN anything.

(Beat.)

PETE: Can we get back to this?

BRIAN: What.

PETE: You know, frankly, I think if we got back to this democracy idea.

BRIAN: *(Hostile, but resigned.)* What democracy idea?

PETE: The one I didn't get to, because you cut me off. *(Starting to pace, spinning.)* Because the point I was going to make, was, that democracy is really something that needs protecting. It's an organism that is so complex and and and vital —

BRIAN: What does that even mean, vital —

PETE: — Let me finish, but its growth has to be managed or it can't sustain itself. For a democracy to be healthy, everyone's voice has to be heard —

BRIAN: Where are we going with this?

PETE: If certain voices grow too loud, they drown out others. And then what do you have?

BRIAN: *(A wild guess.)* Not a democracy?

PETE: Bingo.

BRIAN: *(Simple, getting his spirit back.)* Yeah, except we never had a democracy, in the first place. That's the real problem. Those fucking Founding Fathers —

PETE: What did you say?

BRIAN: Yes, they were a bunch of elitist shits who were too afraid of the stupidity of the common man, that's why they came up with this idiot electoral college —

PETE: OK, this is not where I'm —

BRIAN: And women and blacks didn't have the vote. I mean that's like —

PETE: That's not relevant to what I'm —

BRIAN: *(Overlap.)* It was relevant to them, I'm betting —

PETE: Brian. This sort of thing? Would be considered a a bad attitude. I mean — are we working together here? Or not? You want me to go let people know that your attitude is —

BRIAN: My attitude is fine, I'm just —

PETE: I'm not saying I would. But somebody else might. Come on. You got to let me finish this thought. You just do.

BRIAN: OK, so finish, who's stopping you.

PETE: Democracy, the myriad voices of a democracy need to blend, to harmonize, to be heard in union. Who does the country belong to? Not to any one person, or any one group. It belongs to everyone. Are you writing this?

BRIAN: I am, but —

PETE: When we all listen, to each other, certain chords emerge from the harmony, ideas, ideals, a collective understanding, and agreement —

BRIAN: Where are we going? Are you —

PETE: All over America, people are rising up, coming together, speaking as a community on this.

BRIAN: Yeah, but —

PETE: Uniting on this one issue as they have not united, as a people, behind anything else. Come on, you got to write this down. I'm doing all the work here. America finding its voice, its identity with a clarity and a strength and a conviction that is drawn from the central core of democracy itself: the will of the people.

BRIAN: Pete, listen to me. You're, you're you're talking about about about camps, you know, putting people into — camps —

PETE: Whoa whoa whoa — who said —

BRIAN: You said —

PETE: I said, "specialized housing" —

BRIAN: Yeah, OK, a ghetto, then —

PETE: This isn't 1939, and it's not Poland, either, and your attitude is, I am not kidding —

BRIAN: You said —

PETE: Call it what it is!

BRIAN: Calling it what it is, is what I am trying to —

PETE: *(Overlap.)* A working retreat. No, that's —

BRIAN: *(Overlap, heated.)* You said, hypothetically —

PETE: *(Snapping.)* Look, what is your problem?

BRIAN: My problem — my problem is — that even hypothetically, this is wrong!

PETE: These people have created a very dangerous situation! And it is our job to address that, not to make — excuses —

BRIAN: I'm not —

PETE: — For they way they deliberately undermine the legal system and — frankly — defy justice.

BRIAN: They —

PETE: They defy it.

BRIAN: The rights of —

PETE: Everybody has rights! What about the rights of those Americans who don't want —

BRIAN: Who don't want other people to have rights?

PETE: Seventy percent of those polled, the numbers don't lie. Finally, we can stand up and say, this is not what we are. We know what we are, and we are not you.

BRIAN: Yeah, see but —

PETE: The natural law of the land, a man and a woman —

BRIAN: Yeah, but there's the problem, see —

PETE: This is a democracy. The will of the few doesn't get to decide. And they overreached. They want their voices, their few voices, to drown out the will of the majority. And democracy doesn't work that way. Democracy has a higher purpose than self-interest and social fads. Everybody gets a vote, even if it doesn't count. And they are not allowed to fuck with that. The voices of the few do not get to take over and tell the rest of us what goes. It's not going to happen. It's just not. So you can walk away, or you can get on board with this, now.
(Beat.)

BRIAN: So . . . run it by me again, how do we get from —

PETE: Overreaching, undermining democracy —

BRIAN: Yeah, OK, to, uh "specialized housing"?

PETE: All the demonstrating for their so-called rights. They're demonstrating, right? They violate the law, they go to jail. You put enough of them in jail, and then you segregate them for their own good.

BRIAN: Oh.

PETE: They segregate themselves anyway, they take over neighborhoods and redecorate, all over America, that's what they do. So once you've done that —

BRIAN: *(With sorrowful irony.)* Sure, it's a hop and a skip.

PETE: People want this. I mean, a lot of people, *The New York Times*, will get all whiney about it when it first shows up, but trust me, America wants this. And let me promise you, the powers that be, the boys who sign our checks? They really want it. So stop acting like the world just ended, this is a good idea and you know it. I just saved both our butts.

BRIAN: And we're not talking hypothetical?

PETE: I don't think we have to be. I really don't. *(Beat.)* Write it down!
(Cheerful, he taps the page. Blackout.)

END OF PLAY

DOES THIS WOMAN
HAVE A NAME?

CHARACTERS

SARAH: An actress in her late twenties; pretty in a hometown-girl way, smart, both sarcastic and direct at the same time

MEL: A writer in her late twenties, complicated, introspective

JON: Mel's lover, a lawyer; he wears suits; nice guy

SET

A very bare room, representing Mel's apartment. There are three pieces of furniture: a cot, a table with a computer and printer on it, and a chair. A long sheet of computer paper covered with type spills out of the printer and onto the floor. A telephone with a long cord sits on the bed.

ORIGINAL PRODUCTION

Does This Woman Have a Name? was originally produced at Alice's Fourth Floor in October 1989, Beth Schacter, director, with the following cast:

SCENE I

Lights up on Mel's apartment. Mel sits at the computer, staring at the screen but listening to Sarah, who sits on the bed, talking on the telephone. She holds a pad of paper on a clipboard and writes as she listens.

SARAH: Hi, can I help you? *(Pause.)* That's right, it is. Has Micki explained to you our procedure? Fine. Now why don't you tell me who you'd like to talk to, and what you'd like to talk about? *(Long pause. She scribbles as she listens.)* Uh huh. *(Pause.)* Uh huh. *(Pause.)* Uh huh. *(Long pause.)* Does this woman have a name? *(Pause.)* Uh huh. *(Pause.)* Yes, of course, I'll explain that to her. Absolutely. And can you give me a number where you can be reached in about fifteen or twenty minutes? *(Pause. She writes.)* And who should I tell Inga to ask for? *(Pause.)* All right, Marco. I'll give Inga your message. *(She hangs up.)* This isn't going to work.

MEL: Just let me look at it, OK?

(She holds out her hand. Sarah hands her the pad.)

SARAH: He wants to talk to *Inga.* Inga. I'm sorry, but really, Swedish accents are just not sexy. "Yah, Marco, yah, yah — "

MEL: You have to shut up while I think about this.

(She starts to type rapidly while looking at the notepad. She types.)

SARAH: This isn't going to work.

MEL: What is this, I can't read your handwriting — is this something about a blow job?

SARAH: Yeah, he wants a twenty-four-hour blow job.

MEL: You have got to be kidding.

SARAH: That's what he said. I mean, what am I supposed to do with that? Blow jobs over the phone. Get real. I can't believe guys actually have fantasies about this stuff. I mean, if someone gave me a twenty-four-hour blow job, I'd probably die.

MEL: *(Deadpan.)* But what a way to go.

SARAH: No, I don't think so. Oh, my God, are you kidding? That sounds horrible. Death by a blow job? Oh. Ugh.

MEL: Yeah, but I bet Marco likes it.

SARAH: No. Come on. Are you putting that — Mel, come on. You can't write that. I can't say that; I'll start laughing or something —

MEL: *(Grinning, typing.)* Marco is going to love it. *(She types.)*

(Blackout.)

SCENE II

Lights up on the apartment, the next night. Mel sits at the computer; Jon stands. He wears a trench coat. He sets down his briefcase.

JON: *(Bewildered.)* You're doing *what?*

MEL: It's just for a little while.

JON: Mel —

MEL: I know.

JON: Oh, man. Is it the money?

MEL: Of course it's the money. I just — I can't do office work anymore; it makes me really stupid, and I get home too tired to write; it's pointless —

JON: *(Overlap.)* God, Mel, if you need money, I can give you money —

MEL: I can't take your money —

JON: I make a fortune —

MEL: I can't take any more of your money, Jon! *(Pause.)* And I can't take any more from my parents, either. I mean, at some point, you go, it's time to be a grownup —

JON: You are a grownup! You just sold two stories; it's happening for you —

MEL: *(Overlap.)* I can't live on two stories a year —

JON: You could move in with me.

(Pause. She looks at him.)

JON: OK. Sorry. Forget I mentioned it. You're right. Doing phone sex makes much more sense than moving in with the man you love. I don't know what I was thinking.

MEL: Come on. I just don't think that would solve anything. I can't stop trying to take care of myself.

JON: I'm not asking you to. I'm just saying. You could stay home and write. You're doing so well, I just think if you —

MEL: I am not doing well! I'm completely broke!

JON: You're an artist! You're supposed to be broke!

MEL: Nobody in America is supposed to be broke.

JON: Artists are.

MEL: No, even artists —

JON: Yes, you are. It's romantic.

MEL: Trust me. Being broke is not romantic.

JON: It's very romantic.

MEL: It's a pain in the ass.

JON: It's good for you. You're supposed to live with the poor and record their struggles.

MEL: Yeah, well, the poor don't have parents and boyfriends bailing them out all the time.

JON: But if they did, you can bet they wouldn't argue about it. They'd just say, you want to give me money? Free money? Why, thank you —

MEL: Jon —

JON: I'm telling you, you'll never be an important artist until you learn to say yes to free money.

MEL: *(Pause.)* Jon. I'm not going to take your money.

JON: Mel —

MEL: It won't be for long. I promise. In two or three weeks I can make enough to live for maybe four months. And anyway, it's really not as bad as it sounds. I just write the stuff. Sarah does the actual call.

JON: Sarah? I should have known.

MEL: Don't start —

JON: Was this her idea?

MEL: It doesn't matter who's idea it was —

JON: Mel —

MEL: Could we not fight about this, please?

JON: *(Pause.)* Fine.

(Tense pause. Mel crosses and takes him by the lapels.)

MEL: Come on. Lighten up. There are some benefits to this.

JON: I'll bet.

MEL: Really. Last week I did some job-related research, and I learned some very interesting things.

JON: I'm sure you did.

MEL: I did.

(She pulls his face down and whispers something in his ear. He pulls away, trying not to smile.)

JON: Mel — Mel —

(She pulls him back and whispers again. He starts to laugh, puts his arm around her. She wraps her legs around him. Sarah enters, carrying a shoulder bag and a six-pack of beer.)

SARAH: Ooops. Don't mind me.

(Jon pulls away from Mel.)

JON: Hello, Sarah. How nice to see you.

SARAH: Hey, Jon. So, Mel, doing some warm-ups for our shift, huh?

MEL: Something like that. *(She goes to the computer.)*

JON: So, I hear you two are working together. Congratulations. This whole setup is very enterprising.

SARAH: I know, you think it's sick —

JON: No, hey —

SARAH: It's survival work, OK? I mean, you try being an actress in this city.

JON: I wouldn't want to.

SARAH: I just don't want any shit about it, OK?

JON: I understand.

SARAH: Good. You know, I have to say, you're being pretty open-minded about this. Most guys, I bet they'd freak out if their girlfriend was doing phone sex.

JON: You think so?

SARAH: Oh, yeah.

(The phone rings. They all stare at it for a moment. Pause. It rings again. Sarah picks it up.)

SARAH: Hello?

(Blackout.)

SCENE III

Lights up on Mel and Sarah, Mel on the bed, Sarah sprawled all over the floor, somewhat entangled in the phone, surrounded by streams of computer paper. Sarah holds a strip of paper and reads from the end of it. She speaks rapidly, stream of consciousness style.

SARAH: Yes yes oh yes oh yes oh oh my arms my eyes my breasts oh your tongue oh the soil of the garden slides between my teeth, my saliva moistens it yes I feed you with my tongue in your mouth yes I am transformed into mud my legs my thighs my sex between your legs yes yes OOOOOh. Ohh. Yes. Yes. *(She holds the phone away from her ear for a moment.)* Hello? You OK? You OK there? *(Pause.)* Yeah — yeah, that one got away from both of us. Listen, Sir Michael, we're going to have to wrap up now. Yeah, I'm afraid so. No, it has; it's been twenty minutes — yes, I'm sure. Yes. Yes. OK. Yes. Bye now — Good-bye. *(She hangs up decisively and looks at Mel for a moment, then reads off the paper, expressionless.)* "I am transformed into mud my legs my thighs my sex between your legs yes yes oh oh yes yes." Where do you get this shit?

MEL: James Joyce, Monique Wittig — and some I made up.

SARAH: I don't know, Mel. I think this stuff is a little too creative.

MEL: All you gave me was garden fantasy. That's all I had to go with.

SARAH: I know, but —

MEL: Did he ask for his money back?

SARAH: No.

MEL: All right then.

SARAH: *(Going back over the script.)* Oh yeah, this was my favorite part: "Yes you plant me oh oh your mouth consumes the ripe fruit of my breasts you plow me under you make me earth your tree shoots in my body oh oh oh."

(Mel laughs. Jon enters, carrying a bag with Chinese food cartons and a six-pack of beer.)

JON: It's so nice to see people enjoying their work.

MEL: Hi, hi, hi.

(She crosses and kisses him several times. While they kiss, Sarah starts to open the food.)

SARAH: Plow me. Shoot your tree in me. Yes yes yes. Oh.

(Jon looks at her. Mel pulls away and helps Sarah with the food.)

JON: What is that?

MEL: "That" is Molly Bloom.

JON: That is not Molly Bloom.

SARAH: It's a gardener fantasy.

(She eats. Mel pops a beer.)

MEL: We had a bunch of weirdos tonight, didn't we? The shoe shine guy? And then that guy who wanted to have sex with Joan of Arc?

SARAH: I don't know. I can see that.

MEL: You know, I hate to admit it, but this is kind of fun, in its own weird way. Don't you think it's kind of fun? I mean, I can't believe how easy this is. It's like having the reverse of writer's block. I feel very fertile.

JON: Fertile?

MEL: Fecund. Blossoming. And just for the record, I'm getting a great deal of sick satisfaction out of the fact that none of these guys would take a second look at me on the street because I'm not some sort of live version of a Barbie doll, but I'm the one they come to for their orgasms. I mean it. Phone sex may just be my calling. I feel very fulfilled. I'm writing up a storm, and for once, I'm making a living at it.

JON: So — what are you saying? You're giving up writing?

MEL: No, of course not.

JON: Have you written anything since you started this?

MEL: Jon, could we not —

JON: Have you?

MEL: I was in the middle of a dry spell anyway —

JON: Great. That's —

MEL: Oh, come on, I'm just — never mind.

JON: Mel —

MEL: *What?*

JON: Nothing. Forget it. Sorry. Forget it. *(Pause.)* So, do you ever get any time off from this fulfilling job?

MEL: What?

JON: Don't you get a couple days off once in a while? You guys have been working straight since this started.

MEL: Well —

SARAH: We just did that 'cause we needed the money. But Micki's flexible, we can take a couple days whenever we want.

JON: Good. Then maybe you should do that.

MEL: Jon —

JON: Because one of the partners down at the firm has a house on the cape, which he isn't using this weekend.

SARAH: Why, Jon. What a wonderful idea. I'd love to.
(Jon looks at her.)

SARAH: Oh, chill out. I'm kidding.

JON: What do you say? *(He crosses to Mel, puts his arm around her.)*

MEL: I don't know.

JON: What don't you know?

MEL: I just — I don't know, OK?

JON: *(Coaxing.)* Mel —

MEL: *(Quiet.)* I just don't know.

JON: Come on — *(He kisses her.)*

SARAH: Oh, man — You guys — I'm sorry, but could we not have a public sex scene here? I mean, I'm from the midwest, OK?

JON: Sarah — do you think we could maybe have a little privacy here?

SARAH: I'm hungry!

JON: Sarah —

SARAH: All right. I'm sorry. I'm going.

MEL: It's all right, Sarah. *(She pulls away from Jon, crosses to the table to look at the food.)*

JON: It's not all right, Sarah.

SARAH: I don't know. Doesn't look to me like you're getting anywhere, Jon.

JON: Sarah, please. I'm a desperate man.

MEL: You are not desperate.

JON: I am too.

MEL: You are not.

JON: I am. Can you get the weekend off?

MEL: I said, I don't know.

JON: Great.

(Pause. He sits. Mel stares at the food. Sarah watches them.)

SARAH: So you two are having trouble in bed, eh?

JON: As a matter of fact, we are.

MEL: Could we not discuss very private matters in front of Sarah please?

SARAH: For God's sake, Mel, we have been talking about nothing but the most intimate sexual acts all day. You can't get coy now. So what's the problem?

MEL: There is no problem! I just — when you think about sex all day it's hard to get excited about it.

JON: I have never found that to be true. Back in high school, when I thought about nothing else, I still wanted it. I swear.

MEL: I'm just having trouble relaxing lately, OK?

SARAH: I'm relaxed. I'm horny as hell. I agree with Jon, talking about it just makes me want it. It's like being in a play, you know; this always happens whenever I do a really sexy part. I mean, the guy I'm working with can be a total loser but the stuff I have to say finally gets to me; it's like the script makes me want to have sex. I have had more stupid affairs with crazy actors because of this kind of thing.

JON: Well, maybe you need to set up something with one of your customers.

SARAH: Oh, gross. Jon. That is really disgusting.

JON: You just said —

SARAH: I said, you know, the script makes me want to have sex. These guys on the phone make me want to throw up.

JON: Mel thinks it's noble that you two are reaching out to their humanity. You're touching their souls —

SARAH: Yeah, well, Mel doesn't have to talk to them.

MEL: I didn't say it was noble. I just said it was — I don't know, *real.*

JON: That's not what you said; you said it was your life's calling.

MEL: All I meant was —

JON: What you said was —

MEL: *(Snapping.)* Jon, I know what I said! *(Pause.)* I was just — I was kind of kidding, OK? It just — it's been a while since I had anything published and you get tired of writing for nobody. It feels — different — writing for somebody.

JON: Even if they're sleazeballs.

MEL: Even if they're sleazeballs.

(Pause. She sits and looks at the pages of text, distracted. Sarah eats. Jon watches Mel.)

MEL: I should clean this place up. It's getting — I should just clean it up.

JON: Don't you want some food? You must be hungry —

MEL: No, thanks, I'm not. I'm really not.

JON: I brought all this food —

MEL: I know. I'm sorry. It's great, it's really — I'm just not real hungry. *(She picks up one of the cartons and looks at it. She sets it down. Blackout.)*

SCENE IV

Mel sits at the desk, counting money, which she then puts into a bank deposit envelope. She fills out deposit slip. She is singing lightly, under her breath. Jon lies on the bed, watching her.

JON: They pay you in cash?

MEL: What? No. Sarah gets a check, and she — pays me.

JON: Ah. How much is that?

MEL: Four thousand, six hundred and twenty-three dollars.

JON: Four thousand, six hundred and twenty-three dollars.

MEL: Yeah.

JON: How long did it take you to make that? Three weeks?

MEL: Something like that.

JON: And you're going to quit now? *(Pause.)* You said you were going to quit after three weeks.

MEL: Yeah, well — I don't know. Sarah and I thought if we worked another week or so, we'd both have a kind of buffer —

JON: A buffer.

MEL: Yeah. Look, I gotta go to the bank and deposit this. It makes me really nervous to have it here.

JON: I still make more than you.

MEL: What?

JON: I make more than you. I pull in about two thousand five a week. I told you; I make a fortune. Lawyers make a fortune in this city.

MEL: I know, I just — I didn't know it was that much.

JON: I know. You never asked. I always thought that was weird. We've been going out for almost a year, and you've never asked me how much I made.

MEL: I don't care how much you make.

JON: Sure you do.

MEL: No, I don't.

JON: And you can live on that for how long? Four months?

MEL: Yeah. Yeah, about that.

JON: You're the only person I know who can make five thousand dollars last that long.

MEL: I know lots of people who live on less.

JON: If I gave you five thousand dollars, I wouldn't even feel it. I wouldn't even know it was gone.

(Pause. She does not answer.)

JON: If I gave you five thousand dollars, you'd have ten thousand. You could live on that for six months and still have enough left over to go out to dinner once in a while. Buy yourself some new clothes. Stay at home and finish your novel. Spend some time with your boyfriend. It would be sort of like having a grant, you know, the Jon Diehl Grant for Continuing Achievement in the Arts.

MEL: I'm not going to take your money, Jon.

JON: How come you can take money from these perverts but you can't take it from me?

MEL: I *earn* money from these perverts, OK?

JON: Earn. Right. That is — you are so fucking middle class —

MEL: Could we not —

JON: No, look, I haven't said anything; I've been very good, but this has gone on long enough. When you started this, you said —

MEL: Look, it's my life —

JON: *Take my money. Please. Would you please take my money?*

MEL: NO. *(Pause.)* Look. It just — you have to believe me; it would be bad for us, it would be really bad —

JON: Worse than this?

MEL: YES. I need to take care of myself; that's important to me —

JON: You're not taking care of yourself!

MEL: Look, I'm not going to be your little pet girlfriend —

JON: Don't get feminist on me; you're a fucking whore!

MEL: Get out.

(He looks at her, tries to speak, gives up, and exits. Blackout.)

SCENE V

Lights up on Sarah, on the phone. Mel is on the bed. Sarah reads.

SARAH: *(Oriental accent.)* Yes, under the rising moon I feel you as a gift of the Buddha. You have a beautiful body, Victor-san, which I wash with the tears of all my sisters — *(Pause.)* Excuse please?

(Pause. She stops reading. Mel looks at her.)

SARAH: Yes, Victor-san, I am — uh, moment please — *(She covers the phone. To Mel.)* He's getting all pissed off — *(Into phone.)* Yes, Victor-san, I want to put you in my mouth —

MEL: No, what are you doing?

SARAH: He's all pissed off because it's not sexy enough. *(To phone.)* Yes, Victor-san, oh, oh, you are large and lovely —

MEL: Sarah, stick to the script.

SARAH: *(To phone.)* Yes, Victor-san, I am true geisha — I was raised by Buddhist monks in Beijing —

MEL: No, Sarah, what are you doing? *(She tries to grab the script.)*

SARAH: *(Dropping accent.)* Look, I'm doing the best I can, all right? What do you want here? *(Pause.)* Well, I was getting to that. Yeah, I was, if you would just let me — *(To Mel.)* Write me something, would you? He's losing it.

(Mel hunts for a pencil.)

SARAH: *(To phone.)* Look, would you just calm down for a second —

MEL: Just go back to the script —

SARAH: I can't go back to the script; he knows it's an act. Write me something!

MEL: I can't find a pencil!

SARAH: *(To phone.)* Yeah, yeah, I'm here. Look, Victor, I'm just sitting here thinking how great it would be to — what? *(Pause.)* Look, you don't have to — look — *(Pause.)* What? *(Pause.)* That's really — no, look, you're getting all — LOOK —

MEL: Hang up on him.

SARAH: *(To phone.)* Stop it. *(Pause.)* Stop it.

MEL: SARAH, HANG UP ON HIM.

SARAH: STOP IT.

> (Mel hits the phone, hanging up, then grabs the receiver from Sarah. The two women stare at each other.)

SARAH: Fuck you.

MEL: Sarah —

SARAH: No, fuck you. What the fuck is this shit? You give them all this fancy shit, and I end up — fuck you. You're just supposed to give them what they want. What is the matter with you?

MEL: Why didn't you just hang up on him?

SARAH: You're not supposed to hang up! You're supposed to tell them that they're great and they can do whatever they want to you! Christ, what do you think is going on here? What is this crap, geisha girls —

MEL: He wanted a geisha girl!

SARAH: He wanted to come! *(Pause. She kicks the papers viciously.)* Fuck. I can't believe — I can't believe you're getting a 50 percent cut for just sitting over there and playing games with your little computer while I take this shit.

MEL: Sarah —

SARAH: WHAT? You think it's great; you're having the time of your life dreaming up your little stories; well, it's not so funny when you have to listen to these guys whacking off, OK?

MEL: I'm hardly having the time of my life!

SARAH: Yeah, well you could have fooled me. You don't even need this, with your rich boyfriend —

MEL: That has nothing to do with —

SARAH: He WANTS to support you! Why the fuck are you doing this shit? If I didn't have to, do you think I'd be doing this?

MEL: I don't have a rich boyfriend, all right?

SARAH: Oh, right —

MEL: I don't have a rich boyfriend anymore!

SARAH: Oh, that's just — you are so fucking stupid —

MEL: Oh, shut up —

SARAH: You are so stupid!

MEL: I KNOW!

> (They both sit. Pause.)

MEL: Are you all right?

SARAH: I'm sorry. It's just, some of these guys are really creeps.

MEL: What did he say?

SARAH: Mel, just don't ask, OK?

MEL: I'm sorry.

SARAH: No, I'm sorry. You broke up with Jon?

MEL: I guess.

SARAH: Fuck.

MEL: Yeah.

SARAH: What happened?

MEL: I don't want to talk about it. I'm sorry about this. You're right; the scripts are getting too weird. I'll tone it down.

SARAH: It's not the weirdness. It's just — you gotta keep things sexy, you know?

MEL: I thought that was sexy.

SARAH: OK, then don't keep them sexy. Just keep them gross.

MEL: *(Pause.)* I thought that was gross.

SARAH: OK, then just keep them — disgusting.

MEL: It was about to get disgusting. He freaked out just when it was about to get really, really disgusting.

SARAH: OK, then. Just make sure they stay really, really —

MEL: Repulsive.

SARAH: Appalling.

MEL: Revolting.

SARAH: Filthy.

MEL: Feculent.

SARAH: What? No, now, see —

MEL: I'm kidding. I'll just keep it — nasty.

SARAH: Nasty. That's good.

MEL: Gross.

SARAH: Gross.

MEL: Sick.

SARAH: Sick.

MEL: Disgusting.

SARAH: Disgusting.

    (They look at each other. Blackout.)

SCENE VI

Lights up on Mel and Sarah, Mel at the computer, Sarah on the bed, on the phone. The Chinese food cartons, beer cans, and computer paper from previous scenes litter the stage. A half bottle of scotch stands on the desk; Mel takes a hit from it as she watches Sarah.

SARAH: *(On phone.)* . . . And who would you like to talk to and what would you like to talk about? *(Pause. She writes.)* Uh huh. Uh huh. Uh huh. *(Pause.)* And does this woman have a name? *(Pause.)* Yes, I understand that, but which of these girls would you like to speak to? *(Pause.)* Yes, but if you had a preference — *(Pause.)* I see. I'm sorry, sir, but I assume Micki told you — I mean — well, usually our girls work alone — well, of course, I understand that, but — well, yes sir, we do offer that service, but this just may take a little longer, I have to talk to Micki about this — yes, sir. Well, yes, of course that is a factor. Could you give us your number? We'll call you back in fifteen to twenty minutes. *(Pause.)* And who should we ask for? *(Pause.)* OK, Jean-Paul, we'll call you right back. *(She hangs up and looks up at Mel.)* We got a problem. This guy has a lesbian twin fantasy and he wants to talk to both of us.

MEL: What?

SARAH: He wants two girls. I'm calling Micki; we're not doing anymore weirdos.

MEL: Wait a minute; what did he say?

SARAH: I don't know; he's got some lesbian thing which is totally out of control — I thought the whole point of those lesbian fantasies was that you watched them. Could you tell me why anybody would want to have a lesbian fantasy over the phone? I mean, anybody other than a lesbian. *(Mel takes the pad. Sarah reaches for the phone.)*

MEL: Just hold it for a second, OK? He's willing to pay what? What is this —

SARAH: Triple.

MEL: Triple?

SARAH: Yeah, can you believe that? Four hundred and fifty bucks for phone sex. The things people spend their money on make me sick, they really do.

MEL: God, he must be loaded.

SARAH: I don't care. He could give the money to charity or something. Support the arts. But what is he doing? He's sitting in a hotel room somewhere, thinking about lesbians, and jacking off. The world is in bad shape, I'm telling you. I'm just going to tell Micki I can't do this one.

MEL: You could do two voices. You could do this.

SARAH: Oh, no —

MEL: Yes, you could do that low cigarette voice and then the Betty Boop thing; he'll never know —

SARAH: I cannot — Mel — I can't pull this off. I'm just not good enough, and it's too weird. We agreed, after that geisha thing, no more weirdness.
(Mel takes the pad, sits at the computer, and begins to type.)

MEL: I'll keep it sexy; I promise. Look at it this way: if we get repeat business from this guy, we'll be millionaires in a month. Maybe he'll tell his friends about us.

SARAH: Mel, if I fuck it up, we're screwed; I'm not allowed to hang up again! That other guy made Micki give him the money back —

MEL: Lesbian twins — this is easy; we can do this good twin-evil twin Madonna-whore thing —

SARAH: I can't do it.

MEL: Sarah —

SARAH: *(Real rage.)* WHAT?
(They stare at each other. Pause.)

MEL: *(Quiet.)* Don't you get it? Don't you fucking get it, yet? We can win this. We can beat them at their own fucking game.

SARAH: Man, I don't know what you're talking about, Mel —

MEL: Yeah, you do. We can win this.
(Blackout.)

SCENE VII

Lights up on Mel on the phone, reading from a script. Sarah sits across from her, leaning against the bed; she also has a script in her hands.

MEL: *(Speaking gently.)* I guess I would have to say Sandra's feet are the most beautiful part of her body. She has the feet of a Madonna, and when she slides them over my — oh, ohhhh . . . *(She groans into the phone and hands it to Sarah.)*

SARAH: Yeah, you like that, don't you? Jennifer likes it when I — well, I don't know how to put it. Oh, what the hell. When I step on her. And I don't mind. It feels all right to have her body under my feet. Particularly when I'm wearing my spikes . . .

MEL: *(Writing while she speaks.)* Step on me, Sandra — Ooohhhhh —

SARAH: Just like I'm doing now — *(She hands the phone to Mel.)*

MEL: Oh, don't stop, Sandra — your feet, your beautiful feet — put your feet in me — *(She hands the phone to Sarah.)*

SARAH: Jennifer, yes, yes — let me caress your body with my heels, let me —
Oooohhhh. Oh, I'm sorry, Jean-Paul, this is just getting — it's
getting —

MEL: OOHHHH.

SARAH: Yes, yes, I . . . oh . . . I know, but — it's hard to describe what we're
doing, it's like — it's like —

(Mel hands her a sheet. She reads.)

SARAH: The taste of cold steel.

MEL: Ohhh.

SARAH: *(Pause.)* Blood between your teeth.

MEL: Oooohhh . . . ohhhh . . .

SARAH: One hand, reaching into your chest, under your ribs, holding your
heart until it stops.

MEL: Ohhhh . . .

SARAH: The face of God.

MEL: *(Screaming.)* OOOHHHHH.

(Sarah covers the phone and looks at her. Mel laughs silently.)

SARAH: I'm sorry, Jean-Paul, we got a little carried away with ourselves here.
What? Yes, well — uh huh. Uh huh. *(Pause.)* Uh huh. Yeah, well, I —
just a minute — *(She hands the phone to Mel.)* He wants more.

MEL: What?

SARAH: He wants more, and I'm not dealing with this. You take care of it. He's
got another five minutes or something.

MEL: I can't —

SARAH: Either hang up or deal with it. I warned you about this.

*(She lights a cigarette shakily and turns away. Mel looks at her, looks at the
phone, puts it to her ear.)*

MEL: Jean-Paul? This is Jennifer. Uh huh. Yes, I'm having a great time, I —
oh, yes, I do like that.

*(Jon enters behind them and watches. They do not see him. As she continues,
the words become more and more difficult.)*

MEL: Yeah, why don't you — oh I wish you would — step on me. Are you
wearing spike heels? Oh, yeah, that feels so — *(Pause.)* You want —
OK. OK. Stick it in me. Hurt me. Yeah, I want you to. Put your hand
into my — ribs, I want you to — *(Pause.)* Yeah. Yeah, cut me open.
(Pause.) What? *(Pause.)* Yeah. Um, rip my arm off. Oh, yeah. Make me
bleed. Yes. Stick it in me and tear me open, that's what I want. I want
you to — butcher me. Open. Oh. YES. Hurt me. YES. I want it. YES.
I — *(She holds the phone away from her ear, looks down. Pause. She picks up*

the phone and speaks quickly for a moment.) Sorry, Jean-Paul, your time is up. Bye.

(She hangs up the phone. Silence. Sarah looks at her.)

SARAH: You are something else.

JON: Yeah, she's a remarkable girl all right.

(Both Mel and Sarah jump, then turn to see Jon. He moves into the room.)

SARAH: Jon, for God's sake, you scared me to death. When did you get here?

JON: A while ago. You girls put on quite a show.

SARAH: Oh, that was —

JON: Please. You don't have to explain it to me. It was self-apparent what that was.

MEL: How did you get in?

JON: I have a key, remember? Long ago you gave me this key as a sign of your undying love etc. etc.; we had a little ritual. *(He throws the key on the desk.)*

MEL: I remember.

JON: I thought you might have forgot. I mean, we haven't talked in so long. I wanted to tell you: Your phone must be broken. I mean, I really, I just cannot get through —

MEL: Jon — we're in the middle of our shift, you know —

JON: I know. I wasn't doing anything tonight and I hadn't seen you for a while so I thought I'd come over and watch. You don't mind, do you?

MEL: Well, yeah, I kind of do —

(He picks up the scotch bottle, looks at it, takes a hit.)

JON: So, Mel, you're taking up acting! You're really very good. That was quite convincing.

MEL: Thanks.

JON: Sounded like Jean-Paul enjoyed it a lot.

MEL: He seemed to.

JON: You too. You seemed to be having a lot of fun. It must be fun to actually perform your own work. Makes it a little more real, I guess.

MEL: Well, actually —

SARAH: It was just the one guy. He wanted this lesbian twin thing, and he was offering a lot of money, so —

MEL: Look, I don't have to defend myself —

SARAH: I'm just trying to explain to him —

MEL: I don't have to explain anything, either!

SARAH: You're not explaining it; I am! *(Pause. To Jon.)* It was just the one guy. He said he'd pay triple. It was an offer we couldn't refuse.

JON: I should say not. This is American capitalism at its finest. If you have enough money, you have the right to buy anything. Such as dismemberment fantasies.

MEL: Don't get moralistic on me. You're a fucking lawyer.

SARAH: You guys —

JON: That's right. I'm a fucking lawyer. And as one prostitute to another, I'd like to welcome you to the glorious world of exploitation.

SARAH: You guys —

MEL: There is nothing wrong with what I'm doing! I mean, I didn't invent this game. This is not something my gender needs, you know?

JON: Gender wars! Of course! That's what this is!

MEL: CHRIST, that's what the whole fucking world is!

JON: I'm sorry, I thought we were just talking about phone sex!

SARAH: WOULD YOU BOTH SHUT UP? *(Pause.)* Man.

MEL: I just don't appreciate this, you know? If you have a problem with this, you shouldn't come over here. I'm not going to quit because you're getting territorial about your woman.

JON: Oh, PLEASE. THAT IS NOT WHAT THIS IS ABOUT.

MEL: *(Pause.)* Jon —

JON: I'm sorry. *(Pause.)* I just — it's been so long since we even tried to talk to each other, Mel. Please. Could we just —

MEL: *(Overlap.)* I didn't think we had anything more to say to each other —

JON: Oh, that was it, huh? One fight and that's it —

MEL: It was hardly one fight —

SARAH: You guys, come on, I really don't want to hear this!

(The phone rings. They all stare at it.)

SARAH: Christ. *(She answers it.)* Yeah. *(Pause.)* Oh. Micki, hi — *(Pause.)* Yeah, yeah, that's right, I was about to call you about that; that last guy gets an extra charge — *(Pause.)* He did? Why? *(Pause.)* Now? Christ. *(She covers the phone and talks to Mel.)* Jean-Paul wants a second go around.

MEL: Oh, God.

(Jon starts to laugh.)

SARAH: *(Back into phone.)* He was a real creep, Micki, I'm not doing him again.

MEL: Yes, we'll do it; it's fine. If he wants to fork over another four hundred fifty, that's fine — *(She types.)*

SARAH: *(To Mel.)* What? *(Pause.)* He did? Yeah, well, that's what he wanted; I just gave him what he — No, no, it was just me; I did two voices and —

JON: *(Yelling.)* Don't believe it, Micki! They're pulling a fast one on you!

SARAH: JON — *(Into phone.)* well, yeah, a friend stopped by a few seconds ago, but he's leaving — *(To room, phone uncovered.)* You're going to have to take off, Jon —

JON: *(Yelling.)* I'm not going anywhere!

SARAH: CHRIST. Mel, would you please take care of this?

MEL: Jon, this isn't funny.

SARAH: *(Into phone, overlap.)* I know, Micki, but I'm not gonna do it.

JON: *(Overlap.)* I want one too, Mel.

MEL: Oh, please —

SARAH: *(Into phone, overlap.)* I know. He's leaving —

JON: *(Yelling to Sarah.)* I'M NOT GOING ANYWHERE. *(He pulls out his wallet.)* Come on, Mel, write one for me.

SARAH: You guys, I'm not kidding, could you work this out later?

MEL: *(To Jon.)* For God's sake, could you please not try to teach me a lesson? I don't need this, OK?

JON: I'm not trying to teach you anything; I'm trying to buy myself an orgasm since that seems to be the only way I'm going to get one. Now, can I buy one or not?

MEL: Oh, for God's sake —

SARAH: *(Yelling into phone.)* Yes, I told you, everything is fine here; this is just going to take a little while, all right?

JON: Tell him to call back! They're busy now! *(To Mel.)* So what's the going rate now? Four-fifty?

MEL: Forget it.

SARAH: Just give him to someone else. I need to take care of this.

JON: Here, this is a hundred and something; can I give you a check for the rest? *(He drops a handful of dollars on the desk.)*

SARAH: *(To phone.)* I know that, but —

MEL: YOU'RE NOT SCORING ANY POINTS HERE, JON.

JON: I'M NOT TRYING TO SCORE POINTS, MEL. I'M TRYING TO BUY SOME PHONE SEX.

SARAH: *(Yelling into the phone.)* I REALIZE THAT, MICKI, BUT I DON'T GIVE A SHIT. *(She slams down the phone.)* Now could you tell me what exactly the problem is here?

JON: Are you two running a business or not? My money is as good as Jean-Paul's, and I was here first.

SARAH: *(To Mel.)* Is he kidding?

MEL: Apparently not.

SARAH: Look. I'm just going to leave now. I'm going to leave for an hour and you two can fight or make out or do whatever it is you have to to get this out of your systems.

JON: Are you turning me down?

SARAH: Yes, Jon, I am; I am not going to give you phone sex. I won't do it. *(She heads for the door.)*

JON: You realize of course that it's illegal to refuse legal tender offered in exchange for services which are offered to the general public in the capacity of —

SARAH: *(Overlap.)* Jon, I don't give a fuck!

JON: I'll just go to Micki. This is a business deal; if I can't arrange it through you, I'll go to Micki. Is this her number?
(He picks up the clipboard, crosses to the phone and picks it up. Sarah pulls it away from him.)

SARAH: Oh, man. *(Pause.)* This is cute, Jon, really, but wouldn't you rather work this out some other way? Preferably, some way that does not have me right in the fucking middle of it?

JON: *(Pause.)* This is a business deal. That's all it is.
(Pause.)

MEL: Fine. *(She picks up the clipboard.)*

SARAH: Come on, Mel, please. Don't do this. It's too much. Don't do it.

MEL: And who would you like to talk to?

JON: Joan of Arc. *(Pause.)* Molly Bloom. Scarlett O'Hara. The Virgin Mary. *(Pause.)* You.

MEL: And what would you like to talk about?
(Blackout.)

SCENE VIII

Jon lies on the bed. Sarah sits on the floor, speaking into the phone, reading from a manuscript. Mel sits at the desk, watching.

SARAH: *(Reading.)* Hey baby, how you doing?

JON: Fine.

SARAH: You been waiting for me?

JON: Yes.

SARAH: You been waiting long, baby?

JON: I thought you forgot. I thought you weren't coming.

SARAH: I'm here. I've always been here. I'm just invisible. Didn't you know that?

JON: No.

SARAH: I'm right here, lying right alongside you, my body is pressed right up against yours. Don't you feel me? Don't you feel my hand running down your chest? Don't you feel my breath on your neck? Don't you feel my heat?

JON: No.

SARAH: Yes you do, baby. I'm right here. It's just there's too much heat; we're burning up together and you don't know what's me and what's you anymore. That's all it is. But I'm here all right. My hands are dipping into you; I'm running through your veins. I'm the invisible woman. I made myself invisible for you, so I could be with you all the time.

JON: No. You're never here.

MEL: Just listen.

SARAH: *(Looks at her, continues.)* I think of you all the time. You're all I think of. Ever. The taste of your skin. The feel of your bones. It's all I want. I want you in my mouth. I want you inside me. I want you to make me invisible. Whatever you want, that's what I want. Isn't that what you want?

JON: I want —

SARAH: I know what you want. I know. I'll give you whatever you want. That's what I'm here for. My hands are here. My mouth is here. Underneath you. Down the length of you. My legs winding round you like vines, like roots, like water. I cling to you like water. My hands pass down you like rain. Like blood. Listen, the world does not exist. Only my hands. On you. We grow together. We evaporate. I evaporate. As you emerge.

(Pause.)

JON: That's not what I want. *(Pause.)* You got it wrong. That's never what I wanted. I just wanted you.

MEL: *(Pause.)* You don't know what you want.

JON: I just want you, Mel. I just want you. Mel. Mel.

(Pause. Mel looks at him from a great distance. Sarah looks away. Blackout.)

END OF PLAY

WALK

CHARACTERS
    MAN
    WOMAN

SET
    A bench

ORIGINAL PRODUCTION
    Walk was originally produced as part of "Rebeck Revisited, an evening
    of One Acts presented by Theatre Neo, in Los Angeles, March –
    November, 1999, Mary-Pat Green, director, with the following cast:

    MAN .... Michael Dempsey
    WOMAN .... Rebecca O'Brien

A man sits on a bench. A woman wheels herself on in a wheelchair.

WOMAN: Hi.

(The man looks at her as she nods in greeting, nods in response.)

MAN: Hi.

WOMAN: Is this your bench?

MAN: No. It's not my bench.

(He smiles, polite, and looks out, at the ocean.)

WOMAN: I'm talking a walk. You know, it's weird, you don't take walks. I mean, who in L.A. ever takes a walk? Then one day, all of a sudden, you're in a wheelchair, with a life-threatening disease, and all you want is to, you know, take a walk. Perfect, huh.

MAN: Yeah. *(Looks at his watch.)* Well . . . *(He stands to go.)*

WOMAN: Oh, don't let me drive you off.

MAN: No, you're not. I was going.

WOMAN: No, you were just sitting here.

MAN: Well, now I'm going.

(He starts to go.)

WOMAN: *(Good-humored.)* Oh, that's lovely. I tell you I'm dying and you're like, oh, good-bye. What, are you in show business? You're in show business, aren't you. That's how come you're so sensitive.

MAN: No, no, that's not —

WOMAN: You're not in show business.

MAN: Of course, I'm in show business, but I'm not — look. I have compassion. I do. But I have a lunch.

(He shrugs, only vaguely apologetic. She is slightly taken aback.)

WOMAN: For your information, most people, when they find out that someone is dying, they actually try to be nice.

MAN: *(A little stung, but trying.)* I am being nice, come on. I don't even know you. Right? I mean, right? And come on. I live here, I work here, Los Angeles, you know. I'm trying to be nice. It's just, trouble is not my thing. OK?

WOMAN: I'm with you there. Death isn't really my thing either and yet, I just don't know, I can't get it out of my mind. *(Beat.)* It's fine, go ahead. I'm sorry I bothered you. I just, I thought you were taking a walk. It seemed like a good thing to do. That's what you were doing, right? Taking a walk, looking at the ocean?

MAN: Yeah.

WOMAN: Good.

(She smiles at him and looks away. Now he feels stupid. He waits a minute, unsure whether or not he should go.)

MAN: Are you, you know? Going to be OK here?

WOMAN: Oh yeah, I'm fine. It's so pretty here, isn't it? The sky. I'll tell you, that's something that doesn't get old. Air. You think about things like that, once you, whatever. What's worth your time, and what's not. Like, computer games. If you only had, say, two months to live, would you spend any of that time playing computer solitaire? No. I mean, the answer to that is just, no fucking way. On the other hand, you only have a couple months, you could spend a whole afternoon just look at the ocean. Watching a bird fly in circles. It's weird, huh? You don't think about things like that. Until you're like, you know. Dying.
(Beat.)

MAN: Did my mother ask you to come here?

WOMAN: *(Dry.)* No.

MAN: *(Trying to be halfway nice.)* Sorry, I just — it's the sort of thing she'd do.

WOMAN: No, actually. This isn't about you.

MAN: *(Not getting that.)* So how much — what did you say, two months? That's rough.

WOMAN: Oh no, that was just a, they don't know. I mean, it's not like being on death row, here's your date with oblivion. Now that is something I would not enjoy. I could have years. Not a lot of years, but you know, several, that's a blessing. Well, not a blessing. I actually would not describe what's happening to me like that. I'm sorry, I realize I'm rambling a bit, but ever since this happened to me, I tend to, whatever comes into my head comes right out of my mouth. Pretty soon I'm not going to be able to talk, that's what they — everything shuts down, bit by bit, your neurons stop working, muscle neurons, stuff people like you and I know nothing about, it all just stops working, so they don't know when, but eventually your voice goes, and they can give you one of those throat things that help for a while, or if you still have the use of your hands, you can type, until that goes too. So then you're just in there, apparently, in your head, not able to move or talk or feel or anything. But you're still in there. It sounds like a Beckett play to me, frankly, and to tell you the truth, I never really liked those things, sitting through a Beckett play. It's a nightmare. If I only had two months to live, that's one of the things I would not do. *(Beat.)* You know who Beckett is?

MAN: *(Testy.)* Of course I know who Beckett is. What do you think, just because I'm in the business, I don't — that's so — really. I mean, I'm being nice here.

WOMAN: Oh, you are.

MAN: So, I know who Beckett is, OK?

WOMAN: Ever seen one of his plays?

MAN: Hey, you just said they were boring.

WOMAN: They are.

MAN: So, exactly. Though, I have to say — if you don't mind —

WOMAN: No, I'm interested.

MAN: Harlan Ellison wrote this short story, it's amazing, about this sort of horrible, giant super-computer — malevolent, totally evil, that takes over the world.

WOMAN: Uh huh.

MAN: And it's like, it kills off the entire human race, and then realizes at the last minute, that if it kills off everybody? It'll get bored. So it saves the last human beings, there are like six of them or something, and they just are like toys to this computer —

WOMAN: Like wanton flies to the gods.

MAN: Yeah, like bugs, but really, like toys.

WOMAN: Go on.

MAN: So this super-computer tortures these people for the longest time, and then one of them figures out a way to just murder all the others, to put them out of their misery? And he does it, before the super-computer can stop him. But then he's the only one left, and the computer is so enraged that it turns him into a blob. This blob, you know, that can't feel anything, or say anything, or move, but this person is still in there. Because that's the super-computer's revenge.

WOMAN: *(Beat.)* Wow, that's really —

MAN: It just seemed the same. What you were saying.

WOMAN: *(Simple.)* Yeah, it's — that's weird, it's so the same. *(Convinced.)* My life has turned into a science fiction movie. Now we know. God is a bad science fiction writer.

MAN: *(Honest.)* No, come on, you can't think like that. Like, God would do something like this to you.

WOMAN: Why can't I?

MAN: I don't know.

WOMAN: *(Suddenly bitter.)* Well, you can. OK? You get something like this, out of the blue, believe me, you start thinking about God, and what the hell he could possibly be up to. And you know, the only thing I could come up with, is that perhaps he is trying to make this big metaphoric point. 'Cause this disease, the one I have? Is actually different from Alzheimer's, where the body stays whole but the mind goes, so technically you end up with a person without a person inside. My disease, the body disintegrates but the mind stays whole, so you end up with a person and nowhere to put it! It's a metaphor, see? God is using me to make a point about the lack of spirituality in a materialistic culture. That's what it has to be. There is no other explanation for a disease that would turn my body to mush, leaving me intact, because I'm not my body, I'm me, I'm in here. I'm me. I'm —

(Beat.)

I'm sorry. I think it's not a bad point, the Death of Spirituality in a Materialistic World. But I can't help wishing that God had come up with a different way to make it.

MAN: *(Simple, trying to comfort her.)* I don't believe in God.

WOMAN: *(Knows she's asking the hard question.)* Do you believe in anything?

MAN: Yes, of course.

WOMAN: What?

(Beat.)

MAN: You know, I really do have to go. That lunch.

WOMAN: You like the people you're having lunch with?

MAN: Yeah. They're fine.

WOMAN: Fine?

MAN: *(Defensive.)* The food will be very good. I am not wasting my life, OK?

WOMAN: I didn't —

MAN: You implied it, OK? Did you not just, deliberately — I mean, OK. I'm sorry you're sick, OK? But that's not my fault, and it's got nothing to do with me, and I have to go. I mean, I don't know you! Right? And just because I enjoy myself and don't want to think about death all the time — I admit, I live in Los Angeles and like it, but that doesn't make me a shallow person, OK? And I don't know you. OK?

WOMAN: OK.

MAN: Good.

WOMAN: Believe me. If I'm not going to waste the rest of my remaining time here on Beckett plays, or computer games, I'm certainly not going to spend it worrying about you.

MAN: *(Suddenly furious.)* HEY. I don't need anyone worrying about me! You and my mother, God — this is — God.

(He stops himself, looks down and away. But he does not go. She considers him for a moment, then looks back out at the ocean.)

WOMAN: You know, surprisingly, while there are many things you don't want to do anymore, once you find out your days are numbered, there are some things that you didn't want to do while you had all the time in the world, that now you do want to do. Did that make sense? You know, like you never have time to read poetry because it seems too hard, just too hard, and then, oddly enough, when you're in real trouble, the stuff suddenly makes sense. Shakespeare. Auden. Emily Dickinson. Charles Dickens, he's not actually a poet, but he's written some very good sentences. Time gets short, you don't mind spending it with them. Or that bird out there. It's pretty, isn't it?

MAN: *(Quiet.)* Where? *(He glances up, then.)* Oh, look —

WOMAN: Look.

(They both watch, suddenly amazed, as something unseen happens in the sky. After a moment — .)

WOMAN: (*Continuing.*) Oh, my.

MAN: Oh.

(They continue to watch.)

MAN: (*Continuing.*) Poetry?

(The woman looks at him, surprised, then looks away.)

WOMAN: You should try it.

MAN: Maybe I will. *(Beat.)* I will.

WOMAN: Good.

(They smile at each other for a moment, then turn back to watch the sky. Blackout.)

END OF PLAY

BIG MISTAKE

CHARACTERS

BRIAN: Early thirties, something of a bully
PAUL: Early thirties, confused but friendly
LORNA: Early thirties, stubborn, controlled, intelligent
ANNIE: Early thirties, friendly, talkative
BARTENDER

SET

A bar

NOTE

Because there is so much hostility between the men and women for most of the piece, it is important that the actors play against that hostility with a veneer of politeness and social agility. This veneer is, of course, worn through rather quickly.

ORIGINAL PRODUCTION

Big Mistake was originally produced at John Hooseman Studio Theatre by Jeffrey Seller and Beth E. Smith on May 2, 1991, Arnold J. Mungioli, director, with the following cast:

BRIAN	Christian Baskous
PAUL	Reed Birney
LORNA	Adina Porter
ANNIE	Janine Robbins
BARTENDER	Thom Goff

A small, tasteful bar. A female bartender smokes a cigarette at the bar. A couple of well-dressed young men, Brian and Paul, sit at a table right, sipping beers. An empty table is near the door.

PAUL: I don't know. She's big enough to fucking kill me.

BRIAN: She's not that big.

PAUL: She's pretty big.

BRIAN: She's little. She's, like, five-something, five three or something —

PAUL: She's bigger than that.

BRIAN: She's little.

PAUL: She works out like a fucking maniac. I mean, she's got all those muscles. She's big. Have you ever seen her in that blue sleeveless thing? She could probably break my arm.

BRIAN: I think she looks good.

PAUL: She looks great. I'm just saying.

BRIAN: So don't ask her out. No one's begging you.

PAUL: It's just — it's kind of weird, that's all I'm saying.

BRIAN: I think she looks good.

PAUL: OK, I know, I'm a jerk, I'm a nerd, I can't take the competition, so sue me —

BRIAN: I didn't say that —

PAUL: I just found life a little more comfortable before women spent so much time in gyms. I mean, you had a little more freedom to be an asshole, you know what I mean?

(They laugh. Lorna and Annie enter. Annie is talking a mile a minute.)

ANNIE: So this guy is like pouring me champagne, right, and the fire is going, and he's got like — his place is un-fucking-believable; oriental rugs, antique armchairs, he's even got a fucking Picasso on the wall, I'm not kidding — I mean, I don't consider myself a materialistic person but at a certain point you can't help being *affected,* you know what I mean? — and we're sitting on this overstuffed ottoman-love-seat-fur-futon thing, and his foot is sort of sliding up underneath my butt and moving down my leg, and I'm going my GOD — I mean, I am — my brain cells are about to blow out my ears, you know, my arms have already gone limp, and from this great distance I hear somebody say, "Oh, wow. This is a great movie." And I'm — I go, excuse me? My electrodes are turning to butter, and he's got the TV on. I didn't even notice, right, and they're showing *Nightmare on Elm Street Two* and this guy is suddenly *transfixed.* Catatonic. I mean, I'm going, "Hello. Helllooooo — "

(During this monologue, Lorna takes off her coat and turns to wave to the bartender. She and Brian lock eyes for a moment. She sits down quickly.)

LORNA: Oh, shit.

ANNIE: Exactly.

LORNA: No, I mean, oh shit we better get out of here.

ANNIE: Why?

BRIAN: Oh, shit.

LORNA: Look, could we just go?

PAUL: What?

ANNIE: Why?

LORNA: Don't look, don't —

(Annie looks over at the men. All are suddenly looking at each other. Brian waves. Lorna raises her hand and waves back stiffly.)

ANNIE: You know them?

PAUL: You know them?

LORNA: Yeah. *(She slips her coat off and sits at the table by the door.)*

ANNIE: Look, if you want to go —

LORNA: Forget it. It's too late.

(Brian stands.)

ANNIE: What do you mean, too late, you just stand up and walk out —

LORNA: *Forget it.*

ANNIE: Oh, no. I don't have a good feeling about this.

BRIAN: Hey. Lorna. How's it going?

LORNA: Fine. Hi. Good to see you.

(She holds out her hand to shake. He leans in and kisses her on the cheek. She stiffens.)

BRIAN: Yeah, it's great to see you, too. It's been a while.

LORNA: Yes, it has. You're looking well.

BRIAN: You too. You look good.

LORNA: Thanks. Thank you.

BRIAN: Can I buy you ladies a drink?

LORNA: No. Thanks. We aren't going to stay long.

BRIAN: What can I get you?

LORNA: Really, we're fine. Thank you.

BRIAN: You're not going to let me buy you just one drink?

LORNA: It's not necessary. Really.

BRIAN: I know it's not necessary. That's not why I offered.

LORNA: I'm fine, all right?

BRIAN: I can see that. I just want to buy you a drink.

(Pause.)

LORNA: Thanks. That would be lovely.

BRIAN: White wine, right?

LORNA: Actually, I'm drinking vodka gimlets these days.

BRIAN: Great. Great! I never trust women who only drink wine. *(To Annie.)* And what can I get you?

ANNIE: I think I'd better have a martini.

BRIAN: Great. I'll be right back.

(He goes to the bar. Annie looks at Lorna. During their dialogue, Brian crosses to Paul, and speaks with him for a moment. Paul nods and crosses to Annie and Lorna's table.)

ANNIE: I have a really bad feeling about this.

LORNA: It'll be fine.

ANNIE: We should just go. Now. We should just go now.

LORNA: That would not be wise.

ANNIE: What do you mean, that would not be wise? What is that supposed to mean?

LORNA: I just mean I would prefer not to do anything that might provoke him, OK?

ANNIE: Provoke him to what?

LORNA: Let's just have a drink with him, OK?

ANNIE: Oh, God. So, what, did you sleep with this guy?

LORNA: I would prefer not to talk about it.

ANNIE: I have a really bad feeling about this.

LORNA: We'll just let him buy us the drink, stay for a few minutes, and go. OK? It'll be fine.

ANNIE: You slept with him? How many times?

LORNA: I don't want to talk about it.

ANNIE: More than once?

LORNA: Yes. More than once.

ANNIE: Oh, God.

(Paul crosses.)

PAUL: Hi.

LORNA: *(Smiling but chilly.)* Hi.

PAUL: I'm a friend of — *(He indicates Brian at bar.)* Paul Bishop.

(They shake.)

LORNA: Hi. I'm Lorna. This is my friend Annie.

PAUL: Oh, *you're* Lorna. Nice to meet you! Brian's told me a lot about you.

ANNIE: *(To Lorna, accusing.)* Brian? That guy's Brian?

BRIAN: Here you go.

ANNIE: Lorna!

(*Brian arrives with the drinks as Paul sits.*)

LORNA: Thank you. Brian. This is really lovely of you.

BRIAN: Not at all. I'm just glad to see you.

LORNA: Me too. You look good.

BRIAN: So, you all have made friends already, huh?

ANNIE: Apparently.

PAUL: Have we met? You look real familiar.

ANNIE: I don't think so.

PAUL: No, I'm not kidding. You look like somebody I knew in a previous life, or something.

ANNIE: I don't think I have any previous lives. I mean, I think this is probably my first time around. Or something.

PAUL: Oh. Yeah.

ANNIE: Yeah.

(*Pause.*)

BRIAN: So, what have you been doing with yourself?

LORNA: Not much. You?

BRIAN: Got a new job.

LORNA: Good.

BRIAN: Yeah, I finally just got sick of it at DeCourcey's. I mean, you can only put up with so much shit, you know? You know. I mean, you heard it all. So I finally just told him to fuck off. I'm on my own now.

LORNA: Really?

BRIAN: Well, you know, for the most part. I'm managing a smaller place. In the village. Nobody gives me any shit.

LORNA: Good.

BRIAN: Yeah, it's great. You still with —

LORNA: Yeah.

BRIAN: You are?

LORNA: Sure.

BRIAN: I thought you were pretty sick of it there.

LORNA: It's gotten a lot better.

BRIAN: Sure, but —

LORNA: We had a bunch of meetings about it. It's a lot better.

BRIAN: Yeah, but — I'm sorry. I just thought you were pretty set on getting out of there.

LORNA: I was. But it's gotten a lot better.

BRIAN: Well, good.

LORNA: Yeah.

(Pause.)

PAUL: *(To Annie.)* Are you a lawyer?

ANNIE: Uh, no.

PAUL: Oh. You look like a lawyer. I thought maybe —

ANNIE: No, I'm in retail.

PAUL: Yeah? Where?

ANNIE: Macy's.

PAUL: Maybe that's where I know you from.

ANNIE: You work with Macy's?

PAUL: Well, I shop there.

ANNIE: What do you mean?

PAUL: I mean, I've bought a couple of things there.

ANNIE: So? I mean, what do you think, I'm a sales girl or something? I say I'm in retail, so you think I'm a clerk, or something?

PAUL: No, I just — never mind.

ANNIE: I'm a buyer. I'm not like, a shopgirl on the floor, OK?

PAUL: I didn't mean anything. I mean, I thought you were a fucking lawyer, OK? I didn't think you were a shopgirl. I thought you were a lawyer. I was just trying to figure out why you looked so familiar, OK?

ANNIE: I'm sorry.

PAUL: I'm just, you know — Christ.

LORNA: You guys —

ANNIE: I'm sorry. I just — I am, I'm a little defensive. Look, I don't know you, and I just, I didn't have a great day, so — I'm sorry, OK?

PAUL: *(Chilly.)* Fine.

ANNIE: *(Pause.)* Fine.

PAUL: Christ.

ANNIE: Look, I'm sorry, OK?

PAUL: Sure.

BRIAN: *(To Lorna.)* So, you seeing anybody?

LORNA: Excuse me?

BRIAN: I asked if you were seeing anybody. What, is that too personal or something? I'm just making conversation. I'm just trying to be friendly. You don't have to answer —

LORNA: No, it's fine —

BRIAN: I don't care —

LORNA: Yes, I am seeing someone. Well, a couple people. Nothing too serious.

BRIAN: Oh. *(Pause.)* Do I know them?

LORNA: I don't think so.

BRIAN: What, somebody from work or something?

LORNA: No, you don't know them.

BRIAN: Well, try me.

LORNA: You don't know them.

> *(Pause.)*

BRIAN: OK. Sure. Fine. I was just asking. You know. Making conversation. *(Pause.)* I'm seeing somebody.

LORNA: Well, good.

BRIAN: Yeah, she's great. An actress.

LORNA: Yeah, actresses. They're great. They're always so stable.

BRIAN: *(Pause.)* What is that supposed to mean?

LORNA: It doesn't mean anything.

BRIAN: *(Starting to snap.)* No. I mean it.

ANNIE: Look at the time. God, I'm sorry, Lorna, I completely lost track of things here —

> *(The following two conversations begin to overlap as tempers rise, but should remain distinct until the very end.)*

PAUL: Oh, please.

ANNIE: Excuse me?

BRIAN: I mean it, what is that supposed to mean? Actresses are so stable. What is that?

PAUL: If you want to leave, just leave. Don't make up some cute little song and dance about it. No one's going to beg you to stay.

LORNA: It's just an observation.

ANNIE: Well, thank you. It's been lovely meeting you.

BRIAN: It wasn't an observation. It was a dig.

PAUL: I wish I could say the same.

LORNA: Brian, I don't care who you go out with. I hardly know you anymore. Why would I care?

ANNIE: Listen, asshole, no one begged you to come over and have a drink with us.

PAUL: So excuse me for being friendly.

BRIAN: Oh, you care.

ANNIE: What I can't excuse is your rudeness.

LORNA: Excuse me, but I am not the one prying into my ex-lover's affairs; I don't *care!*

PAUL: *My* rudeness? I ask you about your job and you practically take my head off —

BRIAN: That's right, you don't care, but you just got to make sure that I *know* you don't care; you have to sit there acting cool and superior and hostile —

ANNIE: Look, I just came in here to have a drink! I was in no mood for some stupid male pick up crap —

PAUL: Pick up? Excuse me, honey —

LORNA: *I'm* the one who's hostile? You come over and practically shove these fucking drinks down our throats and I'm hostile. Oh, that's perfect —

ANNIE: Oh, you weren't trying to pick me up? That stupid line about past lives was not a pick up?

BRIAN: If you didn't want the damn drink, then why the fuck are you sitting here? If you weren't even going to be friendly —

PAUL: I thought I knew you from somewhere!

LORNA: Oh, is that the trade off? You buy me a drink so I have to be nice to you?

ANNIE: WELL, YOU DON'T!

BRIAN: YES. THAT'S THE TRADE OFF.

PAUL: THANK GOD.

LORNA: Fuck you.

(Pause. They all glare at each other. Brian and Paul begin to speak almost simultaneously. Their speeches should overlap completely until their finish; likewise, Annie and Lorna's responses should overlap until the bartender cuts them off.)

BRIAN: You women. You don't know what you want anymore, do you? On the one hand you got us treating you like queens, buying you drinks, bringing you flowers, it's all so nice and friendly as long as you're on the receiving end. But as soon as we ask for *anything* — a little conversation, a smile, a little *affection,* God forbid, you got more walls than a fucking prison; you got nothing but attitude and excuses. You keep saying you want a relationship, but as soon as you got one, all you can do is turn us down in bed! You got us jumping through so many hoops we don't know if we're coming or going, and then when we say time out, could someone tell me what's in this for me, you'd think we were threatening rape! Well, it's not going to last, sweetheart. The day is coming when you're all — all of you — you're gonna get yours.

PAUL: *(Overlap with Brian.)* You women. Could someone please tell me what you want from us? I can't talk to any of you anymore; it's like a battle zone around here! I was just trying to have a drink and unwind! I didn't think a reference to past lives was going to start World War three! It was a joke, all right? I was kidding! I was nervous! I don't believe in reincarnation; I barely believe in God. I was trying to start a conversation about something stupid because I happen to know that our mutual friends here would kill each other if we gave them half the chance. I was trying to help. And just for the record, I don't care if you're a sales clerk or a garbage collector or the president of the United States! You looked familiar! I think you're pretty! So sue me!

ANNIE: Listen, asshole, I admit I snapped at you, but you know, I also apologized! You're the one who couldn't get over the fact that I had a bad day. I had a bad day, all right? I had a bad day! And frankly, you caught me at a bad moment. My so-called best friend here had just agreed to have drinks with the most legendary psycho of her sexual past, so at the very instant you started talking about past lives, I was a little tense. I'm still a little tense. You're not helping my tension, all right? I mean, could we just let this go, please? I have a splitting headache and while I might have found you cute at first, you're really starting to get on my nerves. It's time to GET OVER IT.

LORNA: *(Overlap with Annie.)* You can stop crying about what "we" want, Brian; you're not interested in what we want. The only thing you've ever been interested in is what you can get. It's always the same thing with you; we say no, and you say yes, I'm buying you this drink whether you like it or not, and now I own you. The world is so simple, isn't it? You get your way, and when you don't, it's only because we haven't behaved, we're breaking the rules somehow. If you can't control us, it's because we're fucking up, and that gives you the right to do whatever you want. We say no, you say yes; that's rape from start to finish, and we're not the ones who invented it.

BARTENDER: Excuse me. Hey. HEY. *(Pause.)* Look, I know what you're up against, but could you, like, keep things down? Some of us like to pretend we're civilized.

(He exits. Pause.)

PAUL: You thought I was cute?

ANNIE: What?

PAUL: You just said, you thought I was cute. At first. You thought I was cute at first.

ANNIE: At first, yeah.

PAUL: Oh, shit. I know what it is. You remind me of my sister's best friend. Molly. You remind me of Molly. I had a crush on her for eight years or

something. Grade school. High school. Christ. That's what it is. I'm
sorry. That's all it was.

ANNIE: Molly?

PAUL: Yeah. You look just like her. Or you don't, actually, you don't look like
her at all, but you remind me of her. She always looked like she was
either going to laugh or punch you. She was great. I mean, I was two
years younger than her; she didn't even know I was alive, but . . . she was
really great.

(Pause.)

ANNIE: That is so corny.

PAUL: Sorry.

ANNIE: No. No. *(Pause.)* Do you want to have dinner with me?

PAUL: *(Pause.)* Yes.

ANNIE: Lorna?

PAUL: Brian —

*(They turn to look at Lorna and Brian, who seem to not even know they are
still in the room. Pause.)*

ANNIE: Right. *(To Paul.)* We're out of here.

*(They exit. For a moment, Brian and Lorna do not move. They both turn
and look at each other, steely.)*

LORNA: Well. It looks like we have some unfinished business.

BRIAN: Looks like.

LORNA: Do you want to start?

BRIAN: Oh, no. Ladies first.

LORNA: I need another drink.

*(She holds her empty glass out to him. It is a dare. He takes it. They stare at
each other. Blackout.)*

END OF PLAY

DRINKING PROBLEM

CHARACTERS
RENNY: Attractive but somewhat haggard woman in her late thirties, talkative
THE BARTENDER

SET
A bar

ORIGINAL PRODUCTION
Drinking Problem was originally produced at John Houseman Studio Theatre by Jeffrey Seller and Beth E. Smith on May 2, 1991, Arnold J. Mungioli, director, with the following cast:

RENNY .... Ellen Parker
THE BARTENDER .... A. Bernard Cummings

Renny sits at the bar, alone. An empty lowball glass with melting ice sits before her. She finishes a second drink and aligns the second glass carefully alongside the first, then waves the bartender over.

RENNY: I would like another, please. Could I have another? The same.

(The bartender nods and reaches for the glasses. She stops him.)

RENNY: Oh no, could you — could I keep the glasses? I find it helpful to have something to look at. They're a visual aid. I mean, you look at a bunch of glasses kind of lined up, like a little row of soldiers or something, a firing squad, and that has impact. You know?

(The bartender shrugs, pulls an identical glass from behind the bar and pours her a huge scotch on the rocks, hands it to her, makes a note of it on her bill.)

RENNY: Thank you. I appreciate it. You're very kind. *(She looks at the drink.)* You know, these are really the biggest drinks I have ever seen in my entire life. These drinks are huge. How can you afford this? How much do they cost, ten dollars or something?

(He pushes her tab toward her. She looks at it. He cleans as she speaks.)

RENNY: Ah. Yes, I see. That's very reasonable. Yes. Thank you. *(Pause.)* You don't talk, huh? You just — everything is sort of responded to nonverbally, huh? Hey, I respect it. It's a choice. I'm just observing. You know. It's very effective; I can already feel this sort of transference thing going on. I mean, most of therapy — psychology, psychiatry, whatever, the human brain, I think it's a crock, but that transference shit just cuts a little too close to the bone, if you know what I mean. I mean, I'm already — I've been talking to you here for what, two minutes or something, and I'm already projecting all sorts of nasty little thoughts and emotions onto you. Hey, I can't help it, all right, it's just transference, you know, it's a force of nature, it just happens. Like rain or something. Except I don't know, I think that's a crock too, frankly. First of all, "transference" is like the *worst* name for anything; it sounds like "cash register" or something; I just don't know what it means. And second of all — I mean, the main point is — you're completely — you're like a wall, there's nothing there, why shouldn't I think you're thinking all sorts of horrible thoughts about me? Either you're nice or you're not nice. Either you're generous or you're not generous. If you're generous, you smile, or you let your little face crinkle up with sympathy, or you nod or shake your head or something, and if you're not generous, you just sit there with no expression. Because you want the other person to feel like shit, but you don't want to take responsibility for doing that. I'm not saying that's what you're doing. I'm just saying, those fucking therapists don't tell you about that part. *(Pause. She drinks.)* I've never been in therapy. I just think about it a lot. Because I think it sounds like such a great idea: you go and talk to someone about your problems and then your, like, your life is solved. The whole idea just charms me to death. But I can't help it, I just — it seems to me that if it really worked that way, the world would not be quite such a huge mess. So I figure there's a little bit of a scam going on here. That's why I never went into therapy. But I respect people who do. I do. I think that shows a lot of — I don't know, I think it's a very hopeful thing to do. It's like, believing in God. Falling in love. Going into therapy. It's the same sort of thing, you know? Could I have another?

(The bartender pauses for a moment, unsure.)

RENNY: No, I'm not finished. There's still a considerable amount here. Do I have to finish this one before you'll give me another one? Is that like, bartender rules or something?

(He goes and makes her another drink.)

RENNY: I didn't think so. I mean, you see this on television all the time, some guy lining up drinks and then knocking them back one after another . . . not that I'm going to do that. I just want to see what it looks like. I bet it looks kind of nice. We'll have one that the ice is all melted in, one with ice, one half full of scotch, and one completely full of scotch. It will be a variation on my visual aids theme.

(He hands her the drink. She sets it next to the others.)

RENNY: Oh, yes. That's nice. That's very nice. They look like children or something. *(She picks up the half full glass and downs it, then sets it back down.)* And now they're soldiers. *(She picks up the fourth glass and looks at it.)* I don't think this is a good question to ask you at this point in time, but I'm going to ask it anyway. Do you think I have a drinking problem? Don't answer that. *(Pause. She smiles at him.)* You were about to really let loose, weren't you? You were just going to let me have it. But you know, you don't have all the facts. It's very important, when someone asks you a delicate question like that, to be sure of your facts. That's the problem with the world today. Everybody's got an opinion, you know, but they don't have the facts! They just *think* they do. OK. Here's a fact: I hardly ever do this. I mean, I'm sitting here getting wasted for no good reason, and that's not great, but I *never* do this. Hardly ever. But — BUT I do drink every day. Not every day. Almost every day, though. Not a whole lot. A glass of wine before I go to bed, or, you know, a gin and tonic before dinner. And then once in a while at a party, I'll get trashed and then I wake up at five in the morning and feel horrible and hate myself. And that's like, OK, not great, but I don't think that's a drinking problem. I don't. I saw this thing on television about Richard Burton, and *that* man had a problem; he drank like three bottles of vodka a day. Can you imagine? You'd have to get out of bed in the morning and start drinking in the shower or something. I mean, I don't do that. But I do like the way it makes me feel. And that kind of bothers me because you know, there's some part of me that says that life should be enough. You should be able to just be a happy person without this . . . But I have to be frank. Life just isn't enough, all right? And I am very tense. *(She knocks half the fourth scotch back, shudders.)* Oh, God. I'm going to wake up at five in the morning and feel really, really awful. Oh, well. I feel pretty good now. I hate that. I mean, it's like you have to pay for every fucking second of peace you scrounge for yourself, you know? Who made up that rule? One piece of chocolate cake costs like, I don't know, a week of calisthenics or something. And it's not like this for everyone; you see guys shoving down chocolate cake like their lives fucking depended on it and then when I put on a couple of pounds, they look at me like I've killed a puppy or something; whenever a woman gains a couple pounds it's like a moral offense against the universe. You get tired of it, all right? You get tired. It's just, there's so much shit that gets thrown at you. And then when you fight back, when you say, hey, I'm just going to have a piece of chocolate cake, all right, I'm going to have four scotches, it makes me feel better, all right, so fuck you — all fucking hell breaks loose. You wake up at five in the morning, wishing you were dead. And it's not your fault. It's not my fault! It's like that Chinese water torture, you know, one fucking drop isn't going to drive you out of your mind, but you know, number 8,712 is not so funny! That's all I'm saying, all right? That's all I'm saying!

(Pause. They look at each other. The bartender is clearly listening to her, and has been for a while.)

RENNY: You see? Now you're listening. Now I can see you're a real person. You don't have to say anything. That's not what I wanted. This is what I wanted. This is all I ever wanted.

(They stare at each other for a long moment. The lights fade.)

END OF PLAY

CANDY HEART

CHARACTERS
MONICA
BRENDA
BARTENDER

SET
A bar with several small tables

ORIGINAL PRODUCTION
Candy Heart was originally produced at Alice's Fourth Floor on February 14, 1992, Beth Schacter, director, with the following cast:

MONICA .... Gayle Keller
BRENDA .... Kristine Nielsen
BARTENDER .... .not available

A bar, with a bartender behind two women, Monica and Brenda. They sit at a small table that holds two glasses, a bottle of scotch and a bag of Brach's candy hearts. As Monica pours two large glasses of scotch, Brenda holds up the hearts and reads them carefully, one by one.

BRENDA: "Be mine." "Cute gal." "Some babe." I can't believe it. Even these little candy hearts are sexist.

MONICA: Oh, please don't start.

BRENDA: What? It's true.

MONICA: I don't care if it's true or not. I don't want to have a discussion about it. I just thought it would be nice, you know, little candy hearts on Valentine's day, it's a holiday, we celebrate, so I bought the candy hearts, all right?

BRENDA: You don't have an opinion on this?

MONICA: No, I don't have an opinion. I think it's stupid so I don't have an opinion.

BRENDA: "Some babe" is not sexist?

MONICA: I don't care if it is or not.

BRENDA: "Be mine" is not sexist.

MONICA: Brenda —

BRENDA: What? It's not a big deal. I mean, I'm not the one making a big deal out of this. I'm just making an observation. "Be mine" seems sexist to me.

MONICA: That's the stupidest thing I ever heard.

BRENDA: Oh, "Be Mine" is not sexist?

MONICA: No, I don't think it is.

BRENDA: It's completely sexist. "Be mine." Let me own you.

MONICA: It's a candy heart!

BRENDA: Please. Don't be so naïve. In a sexist culture, everything has a sexist point of view.

MONICA: Oh, my God. Could we not do this tonight? I mean, it's Valentine's Day. Could we just not do this?

BRENDA: Valentine's Day is the most sexist thing of all.

MONICA: Could we please not —

BRENDA: The whole thing is a male plot to make a woman feel stupid if she's not some cultural object of desire. I mean, look at the two of us. Is this pathetic or what? We're so depressed about being single we came here to get drunk.

MONICA: I know, Brenda. I know. Which is why I really think we should be

nice to ourselves. You know, not argue. Laugh. Have a drink. Make ourselves feel better.

BRENDA: We should rewrite these little fuckers. That'll make me feel better.
(She rummages in her purse for a pen.)

MONICA: I have an idea. Why don't we just eat them? Yeah, it's perfect. We
take that fucking sexist message and chomp on it. Chew it up. I think
we have to. It's the only politically correct response.

BRENDA: Are you kidding? It would be like, ingesting the male point of view.
No thank you. Besides, have you ever had one of these? It's like eating a
piece of chalk. I thought the whole point of candy was that it tasted
good.

*(She is scribbling on the little hearts. Monica sips her drink and watches her,
disgusted, then speaks, mostly to herself.)*

MONICA: You know, this really, this was not how my life was supposed to turn
out. By now, I was supposed be settled. I was supposed to have a house,
you know, filled with things, beautiful things that I loved, and my career
was going to be sailing along, like a tidy little ship, not yet arrived at it's
destination, but getting there, on it's way, and in the evening I would
read books and go to the theater and I'd study languages in my spare
time and I'd play the piano and travel, to, to Egypt and China and
European cities, and I would always eat delicious food but I would never
get fat. And I know it's absurd to think of your life that way, but I always
did, and the weird thing is, there was never a man in it, not specifically,
I mean, or even, really, not at all. I mean, of all the things I dreamed of
having, I never dreamed of a husband, all I ever pictured was the occa-
sional date with some fabulously interesting movie star, Jeff Bridges, say,
who I would have great sex with, but who would mostly leave me alone.
When I thought about my life, a man was never anything I had to have.
Then I grew up. And not only do I not have any of that shit — I'm
lonely. *(Pause. She drinks.)*

BRENDA: Here. This is better. "Up yours." "Fuck you." "Eat me."

MONICA: What?

(Brenda licks the back of one and sticks it to her forehead.)

BRENDA: I'm going to turn myself into a Valentine for America. Here, you can
have one too. This is a good one. "Fascist state."

MONICA: What? What does — what does that mean? It's Valentine's Day!
What does "fascist state" have to do with Valentine's Day?

BRENDA: Well, you know, we live in a patriarchal fascist state. Men are fascists, and women are scapegoated and men are trying to control our bodies in the name of love. Fascist state.

MONICA: I can't believe this.

BRENDA: OK, that one's a little too political for you. You can have this one.

MONICA: *(Reading.)* "Screw sex."

(Brenda is trying to keep the little hearts stuck to her face. It doesn't quite work.)

BRENDA: Oh, fuck me. Do you have any scotch tape?

MONICA: No.

BRENDA: Oh, well. Fuck it.

(To keep them on, Brenda has to balance them on her face, which she holds up to the light.)

BRENDA: Here I am, America! This is what I think of your fantasies of male superiority and domestic bliss. *(She stands and walks around carefully, balancing the hearts on her arms and face. Singing.)*

"Here she is, Miss America . . . "

MONICA: Oh, Jesus.

BRENDA: I think I look good. What do you think?

MONICA: Fabulous. Fascinating. You're really just letting them know where you stand. Yes sir.

(Monica is about to eat her candy heart. Brenda stops her.)

BRENDA: No, no, what are you doing? You can't eat them! These are our messages to the world!

MONICA: Oh, for heaven's sake, Brenda, I mean, this is — could you just have a drink. My God.

BRENDA: Come on. Only eat the ones that I didn't rewrite.

MONICA: What?

MONICA: Only eat the ones that I didn't rewrite, please. If you have to to chomp on something, chomp on the male point of view.

MONICA: What if I want to chomp on the female point of view?

BRENDA: Come on, I'm not kidding.

MONICA: Why is this turning into a major crisis? I just want to eat a fucking candy heart!

BRENDA: Why do you want to eat them? They taste disgusting. If you wanted candy, you should have bought chocolate or those chewy red things with sugar all over them.

MONICA: I didn't want chocolate or red things. I wanted candy hearts.

BRENDA: Oh, what, you had a craving for candy hearts?

MONICA: Yes, I did.

BRENDA: You did not.

MONICA: YES, I DID.

    (And she eats it.)

BRENDA: Oh, for God's sake — Monica —

MONICA: What?

    (She eats another.)

BRENDA: Oh, Jesus —

MONICA: I bought them. I'm going to eat them. Oh, look, here's a good one. "Boys suck." Ha ha ha. How witty.

    (She eats it.)

BRENDA: Fuck you.

MONICA: Oh, yes, we have one of them, too. *(She pops it in her mouth.)* Mmmmm. Dee-licious.

    (Brenda stares at her. Monica stares back and munches happily.)

BRENDA: It's good, huh.

MONICA: Wonderful.

BRENDA: Well. Then maybe you should have another.

    (She takes one off her face and pelts her with it. Monica stares at her, then sticks another one in her mouth. Brenda throws another at her. Monica eats another. Brenda throws another. Monica eats. Brenda crosses back to the table and takes a handful. Monica stares at her. She reaches into the bag and grabs a fistful herself. The two stare at each other for a long moment. Blackout.)

END OF PLAY

AFTERMATH

CHARACTERS
DENISE

SAM

SET
A couch in a room

ORIGINAL PRODUCTION
Aftermath was originally produced as part of "Couchworks" by Slant Theatre Project, presented by The Tank, in August 2005, Josh Hecht, director, with the following cast:

SAM . . . . .Brian Slaten

DENISE . . . . .Makela Spielman

Someone lying on the couch, face down. Denise walks through, annoyed as shit.

DENISE: This place is a pit. *(She goes off, messes in the kitchen. Continuing; offstage.)* It's a fucking pit! It's disgusting! Hellloooo! I am not doing these dishes!
(Sam enters. He is half awake, yawning.)

SAM: God what a pit. *(He looks at the body on the couch, nudges it.)* Hey. *(Nudge.)* Hey. *(Nudge.)* Hey. *(Looking about.)* What a pit.
(Denise crosses through again.)

DENISE: Oh look who's up.
(She goes off in the other direction. Sam goes to the kitchen.)

SAM: *(Offstage.)* Oh God. *(Reentering.)* Christ God almighty the kitchen is a mess! Are you, have you seen the kitchen?

DENISE: *(Offstage.)* Yes, I saw it!

SAM: Jesus God above. Oh God. Oh. My head hurts. *(Yelling.)* Do we have any orange juice or anything? Oww.

DENISE: I can't hear you!

SAM: Jesus. I need a coke or something with bubbles in it. *(To person on couch.)* Hellloooo. Hey. *(He touches the guy's foot.)* Hey. *(Nudge.)* Hey.
(Denise reenters, with purse.)

SAM: *(Continuing.)* Are you going out?

DENISE: Yes I am.

SAM: The kitchen is a . . .

DENISE: Yes it is.

SAM: If you're going out can you get me some coke or something?

DENISE: I'm not coming back until I don't know when I'm coming back, all right?

SAM: Well, where are you going?

DENISE: I'm going to have brunch with Lisa, and then we might do some shopping, I don't know, or see a movie, I don't know.

SAM: Well then so you you might come back sooner, right?

DENISE: I don't know.

SAM: I just could use some coke or something.

DENISE: If I think about it I'll get it.

SAM: Well what are you so mad about?

DENISE: I'm not mad.

SAM: Oh fuck you you are too.

DENISE: I'm not mad! I'm just a little put out, you and your friends as you may have noticed did quite a number on —

SAM: Oh now they're my friends.

DENISE: They certainly aren't my friends —

SAM: You were here too —

DENISE: I was being polite.

SAM: You were trying to get laid, is what I think you were trying to do.

DENISE: I was, excuse me what did you say?

SAM: Never mind. Ow. Never mind.

(Beat.)

DENISE: When I come home, this mess better be cleaned up. And that includes your friend on the couch.

SAM: Oh stop it!

DENISE: And that means the kitchen too. I'm not the fucking maid.

SAM: You were the one, you said, why don't I invite —

DENISE: Oh no no —

SAM: Invite Stu AND Dennis AND John, for a couple of drinks —

DENISE: A couple of drinks at eight P.M., not five AM Not thirty-two people at —

SAM: That was on you, you were the one —

DENISE: You are so full of shit —

SAM: The whole thing was your idea! You wanted to get laid, so you had this brilliant idea, bring all my friends over so you can — do whatever, whatever —

DENISE: *(Overlap.)* I was trying to be nice to you and your stupid friends and you do nothing but take advantage this is not your fucking fraternity house, this is my home, and I pay the rent —

SAM: I pay rent!

DENISE: Two hundred dollars every third month isn't rent, Sam! That's pretend rent!

SAM: I pay more than that.

DENISE: You fantasize that you pay more than that but I'm the one who —

SAM: I'm not fantasizing anything, my head hurts too much for me to fantasize, I'm telling you, I pay rent, every month, sometimes I'm a few days late but —

DENISE: A few days late, that's hilarious —

SAM: It's not hilarious, it's true, you're insane, I pay my share of the fucking rent!

DENISE: I am not arguing about the rent!

SAM: Yes you are you're the one who brought it up! You said, you pay the rent so that gives you the right to suddenly I guess totally fuck with reality and pretend that the facts are whatever, totally not what the facts are, it's like living in a fascist state around here. I said this, you said that, and then you're like no it's something else entirely and I'm right because I pay the rent. When I pay rent too. It's just insane. What planet am I on? *(Beat.)*

DENISE: You're on Planet Fucked. Because if I come back in three hours, and this place isn't spotless, all the dishes done, the counters wiped off, the floors vacuumed, the vomit in the bathroom wiped up and disinfected, if that's not done, and your little friend here is still sleeping on my FUCKING COUCH, WHICH I PAID FOR, I am tossing your stuff out the window and changing the locks on the doors. You want to see a fascist state? Stick around.

SAM: Yeah see that's how fucked you are.

DENISE: No Sam, it's how fucked you are.

SAM: I don't know this guy, Denise! And you're the one who slept with him! So you get rid of him!

DENISE: I didn't sleep with him!

SAM: Fuck you.

DENISE: Fuck you! I don't know who that is! That's one of your insane friends, and I want him off my couch!

SAM: That's not one of my friends.

DENISE: It is too, he came with, he came with —

SAM: I don't know him!

DENISE: You don't know this guy.

SAM: No, I don't know him. You knew him. You slept with him.

DENISE: Stop saying that.

SAM: I saw you, I saw you take him into your bedroom at one AM —

DENISE: *(Overlap.)* That is utterly insane. Are you crazy? That is a complete and utter —

SAM: *(Overlap.)* And neither one of you came out until I went to bed at six!

DENISE: — Lie, you were so fucking shitfaced by one AM, there was literally no way for you to see anything! How would you know?

SAM: I'll tell you how I know it's because I saw it, that's how I know.

DENISE: Because you were watching me, is that how you know?
    (Beat.)

SAM: I wasn't watching you.

DENISE: Then you don't know anything.

(Beat.)

SAM: I saw you.

DENISE: What are you accusing me of, Sam?

SAM: I'm not accusing you of —

DENISE: It sounds pretty much like a fucking accusation —

SAM: You want to sleep with some guy, some fucking guy you don't even know his name, be my guest.

DENISE: I didn't sleep with him.

SAM: Then who was it?

DENISE: Why do you care?

SAM: I don't care. I don't care. You're a fucking fascist, sleep with whoever. I don't care.

(Beat.)

DENISE: I didn't sleep with anybody.

SAM: Then who'd you go in there with?

DENISE: I don't — Stu maybe, he needed to use the phone at one point and it was loud, you know, so . . .

SAM: You were in there a long time.

DENISE: I went to bed. After Stu used the phone, I . . .

SAM: He just used the phone?

DENISE: Yes. Yes! *(Then.)* Were you watching me?

SAM: I wasn't . . . my fucking head hurts.

(Denise sets her purse down. She goes into the kitchen. Returns a minute later with a wet washcloth, puts it on his head.)

DENISE: Does that help?

SAM: It's a washrag.

DENISE: So?

SAM: So, my . . .

(He puts his hand on her hand. He reaches up and kisses her, sudden. They start to make out, on the floor. It gets quite involved. They stagger up, toward the couch, fall on the guy. Denise screams and they both back away from the couch. After a moment, Sam laughs, goes and shakes the guy's foot.)

SAM: Hey. Hey, you got to get out of here. Hey.

(He shakes the guy's foot. There is no response. He looks at the guy's face.)

SAM: *(Continuing.)* You really don't know this guy?

DENISE: Never seen him before in my life.

SAM: I don't know him.

DENISE: Hey. *(She goes and shakes his shoulder.)* Hey. *(Shake.)* Hey. HEY. *(She looks at him. After a moment, something changes in her demeanor.)*

DENISE: (*Continuing.*) Shit.

SAM: What?

DENISE: (*Tentative, touching him.*) Hey.

> (*She leaps back, away from the body on the couch. She is suddenly horrified.*)

SAM: What? What?

> (*They look at each other. He gets it.*)

SAM: (*Continuing; looking at body.*) What?

> (*Blackout.*)

END OF PLAY

ART APPRECIATION

CHARACTERS
MISS PAULA

SET
A chair, and an easel, with a painting on it

ORIGINAL PRODUCTION
Art Appreciation was originally produced at the 4th Annual Boston Theater Marathon (sponsored by Lyric Stage) in April 2002, Spiro Valudis, director, with the following cast:

MISS PAULA ....Paula Plum

Art Appreciation was previously published by the *Harvard Review.*

Miss Paula stands beside an easel, on which a painting has been placed.

MISS PAULA: People have a lot of questions. It's been a cause for concern, for many many years now. And pain. I know that some people are worried, distressed — truly distressed, deeply, anguished even. I feel that. I really do. That's why I feel — I just have to say — to put everyone's minds at rest — I have it. The Vermeer? From the Gardner? *(She points sideways, at the painting.)*

I have it. *(Looks at it.)*

And I have to tell you — It's really beautiful. *(She laughs.)*

Truly, truly. You can stop worrying, it's in good hands, because I love it. *(She laughs.)*

Do you want to see it? *(She makes to turn it around.)*

Just kidding. I mean, I'm not kidding that I have it, I'm kidding that you can see it. Of course you can't see it. What would be the point of stealing a Vermeer if you were just going to show it to everybody? I mean, if I were interested in sharing my Vermeer — I like the sound of that, "my" Vermeer. "My Vermeer," — anyway, if I were interested in sharing my Vermeer, I would just give it back. Wouldn't I? I would like, roll it up, stick it in a tube and FedEx it to the Gardner, boy that would make the papers. All over the world! People would be talking about that for a looong time, in hushed tones, the wonder of it, the mystery: The Vermeer was gone for years and years, and then it just showed up one day, because some anonymous art lover suddenly remembered a deep truth lost in the distant echoes of time itself: Sharing is good . . . *(She laughs.)*

No, no, I'm not making fun of sharing. What kind of person do you think I am? *(She laughs again.)*

I'm just saying, sharing and art are not necessarily two words that often appear in the same sentence. Look, let's face it, when old Isabella Gardner bought the damn thing, sharing was not exactly on her mind. She wasn't thinking, oh cool, I've got a Vermeer now, let's hang it in the window so everyone on Comm Ave. can see it. No no no, she was thinking, I have a Vermeeeeeer. Now me and my favorite friends can look at it whenever we want, and no one else can, unless I say so. When I die, maybe I'll let people look at it then. Yes, I think I will. They can come to my house and look at my Vermeer, so long as they can afford the rather exorbitant entry fee. Look, I'm not criticizing Saint Isabella. Far from it. She is my hero. We are a lot alike, you know. You know, she was a vibrant and passionate lover of art, and lover of artists but she also suffered from depression, her whole life. She really struggled with it, sometimes it would come on her and overwhelm her, and she would have to take long fabulous European vacations to get over it. I suffer from depression, too. It's true, and I'm telling you, it's no joke. When you fall into it? It's completely overwhelming. You just don't know how to get out, it's like being trapped inside your own mind, spinning into ever darker places, and you know, that somehow, this isn't true, what you see and feel about yourself and the world, that the world is a bigger place, full of light and hope, and meaning, but all of that is so far from you, and it's virtually impossible, simply impossible to know how to climb out of your own despair. Nothing helps.

Well — having your own Vermeer, helps a little. *(She laughs.)*

OK, it helps a lot. The surest fix I know, when things are getting a little gloomy, is to just sneak a peak. Let me demonstrate. *(She looks, admires, puts her hand on her heart.)*

Well, I do; I feel a lot better. No kidding, this painting is very satisfying to look at. It fills my spirit with so much reverence for humanity, for beauty and light — one of the purposes of art is to ennoble the human spirit, and I can feel that happening, when I look at my Vermeer. I feel really noble. *(She laughs.)*

Well, I do, but it's not like I don't understand the irony of my situation. You own your own Vermeer, that's the sort of thing that helps you keep things in perspective. Sure, I'm out of work. But I have a Vermeer! OK, my boyfriend dumped me. But I have a Vermeer! I hate my landlord, my thighs are fat, my bank account is nonexistent, but . . . See how it works? It's a palliative, to life! It is a cure for all woe. I had always heard that art could do that. But it wasn't until I owned my own Vermeer that I understood how deeply, literally true that was.

So stealing a Vermeer — not that I stole it, I'm not saying that either — and I'm not absolutely admitting I have it either, that's the other reason I can't show it to you, plausible deniability is absolutely essential in cases like this — but hypothetically, let's say, stealing a Vermeer would not necessarily be a transgressive act. Well, it would be transgressive, but my point is, all art is transgressive, isn't it? Artists live transgressive lives, no one wants their kid to grow up and be a painter or an actor, God forbid, your kid says "I want to be a playwright," and you want to blow your brains out. It's just not a wise thing, being an artist, well, there's potentially wisdom in it, but potentially madness too, in equal proportion. Maybe even more madness than wisdom, that would depend on how stable you are, and how stable is any artist? Are you following this? 'Cause I'm not entirely sure I am, but I also think I may be onto something. The fact is, artists make the culture very nervous. They're always saying or doing upsetting things, for no money. Which, let's face it, makes people want to hit them, the critics are always so upset and angry and mean, you got to think about that, critics are people who see art all the time and it seems to have made them a little nuts too. It certainly has made them angry.

So here we have these artists, flailing around, making beautiful things that also seem to upset people, people are embarrassed if their kids become artists, critics want to beat them up all the time, and they're constantly broke unless they hit the big time, which even Vermeer didn't do, so hitting the big time isn't exactly what makes a person an artist. What is my point. I'm not sure. No. I have a point! My point is, as far as the culture is concerned, artists and what they do, all of that is really just one step away from criminality and madness. Vermeer was nuts, the way he lived his life was nuts, he had ten kids, and he took years to paint these things, and then he couldn't sell them. What he was doing with his life, by all modern American standards, was completely insane. He died a pauper. They had to auction off all his work, to pay his bills. He left that family of ten kids in utter destitution. He was, in short, a complete loser. A talented, brilliant, visionary loser. I feel an affinity for that. I feel that by claiming this Vermeer as my own, I am celebrating his transgressive essence. And creating my own little work of art. By stealing it. The way he stole light. The way he stole earrings, and faces, a blanket on a table, a glass of wine, a servant girl. The way he stole windows and maps, on walls, and desire, and a red hat.

He was a thief, he stole life in the name of art, and we revere him for that. And that is why, I'm not saying I did steal it. I'm not making any admissions, remember. But I will say, I wish I did. *(Toying with them again, for just a moment.)*

In my heart, I hope I did. Because there, when I look at it, I can be with it, in its essence, as I remember what it means to be human, in all its greatness and sorrow and beauty and insanity. *(She turns and looks at it. Her face lights up with appreciation.)*

It's really magnificent. It really just is.
(Lights fade out as she cherishes her Vermeer.)

END OF PLAY

JOSEPHINA

CHARACTERS
JOSEPHINA

ORIGINAL PRODUCTION
Josephina was originally produced at the 3rd Annual Boston Theater
Marathon (sponsored by Hartford Stage) on April 8, 2001, Nina
Steiger, director, with the following cast:

JOSEPHINA . . . . .Maria Gabriele

Josephina, at the kitchen table. She is drinking coffee. There are papers spread before her. Piles and piles of paper around her.

JOSEPHINA: I have written a diary, too. In times of crisis. The world is changing around you in ways that no one ever imagined, like lightning, life is suddenly unimaginably not itself. Many of us began to write. In secret. Secret almost from ourselves, at least that is the way I first saw it. It is not in my nature, I don't know for anyone who this is a natural act, frankly, but we all become like squirrels, suddenly, hoarding our lives like nuts in the wall. That is how strange everything had become. Now there is time, placed on top of everything that happened, so everyone, all of you who are even now too afraid to write, now with your time, you think you know everything. How it happened. How it was. How people did what they did. But we who lived through it, we had no choice but to write down events as they happened, without knowing what their meaning would be. Some of you were not born then, some of you are not even now, even so, even so you tell yourself that you have special knowledge. You know. Without the writing of it. This is supreme arrogance. You know nothing, other than what we give you, what we lived and wrote and stored in the walls of our cities. We had the living of it. This you cannot know unless you read, and even then, even then, you know, well. Nothing. *(She shakes her head and looks at the pages before her, starts to pick them up, pour through them. She lights a cigarette and smokes, as she tries to explain her meaning.)*

Why do I bother. Yours is a stupid time. They tell me people do not read anymore. There is too much comfort, around you, you are so distracted with money and food and desire, you cannot read, and so you cannot think! I heard this from one of your people, he talks about your time as being more "sophisticated," this he said to me, "People are more sophisticated now, so you have to tell the story quickly, your story is too complicated." How is this sophisticated, I ask him? People are sophisticated but they cannot think? He said, on the contrary, they think quickly. People now, so much is given to them by the world, with their television and computers and shopping that they are very smart and very fast and very sophisticated. I said, oh, because where I came from sophisticated meant that one was knowledgeable. Capable of thought, of shrewdness, patience, survival. It did not mean thinking you knew everything so quickly that you didn't have to listen with care. In my time, if you did not listen with care, you were dead. We were an occupied country! Soldiers, everywhere, men with disaster in their faces, you didn't know what they could do. They could do anything. Rape, yes, theft, destruction, arrest, and whatever then came with it, death, the camps, you were better off if they just killed you. We all knew that. And this walked among us. I cannot tell this story quickly. What it means to have men like that walk among you. Because it is fear of that — deep fear, the mystery of what we are capable of becoming, before you, knowing you do not exist before that — that fear is not cowardice. The Nazis. You cannot talk of them quickly. If you talk of them quickly, you forget the one true thing, which is that it happened, which also means that it will happen again. *(She stops, making sure that they have heard her point, then goes back to her pages.)*

You think it not present in your fast, sophisticated world, but it is there. And let me tell you something funny about the Nazis: nothing. There was nothing funny about them. To a man they had not a shred of humor among them. That goose step was funny, and if you really looked at the haircut on that man, sometimes Hitler could be funny too. But overall, it was terror, do you see? You don't understand terror anymore. You think in your small way of the dreams that rise unbidden, at night, spooks from your television sets, tales from another land. We had the real thing, enter our homes in the dead of night, men in black uniforms, crashing down the door of your bedroom at one or two or three in the morning, dragging you from your home, screaming in rage, beating you with clubs, for what? They do not say! Your children sobbing with fear, you cannot go to them, neighbors turning away, knowing that even the sight of you in your nightclothes, in the hands of such men, the seeing of you in the throes of your terror will bring down the same fate on them.

It came to be, with time, that this madness was not mad, it was commonplace, it was the natural state of affairs. Peace, kindness, gentleness, humor, this was the dream. We would whisper to each other, on the streets, did you see, did you hear, last night, has anyone seen him since? The rumors that were about, of what was happening elsewhere, the whole world infected by a murder so large, the bodies of men and women and children, their bones, burning everywhere, millions covering all of Europe with the smell of not death, but murder. Murder. And the thought of that, the knowledge of it, coming into your mind? The very knowledge was dangerous. The writing was dangerous. Keeping a history of the dementia, this was a treasonous act. They had their fingers in your brain, finally, do you see? Breathing itself was potentially treasonous. You knew that. And, you were starving. Your children were starving. Do you know anything of this, in your fast, sophisticated world? How sophisticated you all are, you don't have to know! *(She sits, looks at her papers.)*

The price for a Jew was seven-and-one-half guilders. Each. I knew there was more than one. How many, it was impossible to say. There had been rumors, in the neighborhood, that Frank was in there, with his whole family; if true, that meant at least four. Thirty guilders at least, enough for us to live, to eat, for two entire months. Then to be told, afterwards, there were eight. Sixty guilders! And the money was only half of it. To have brought eight Jews to them. To be an informant, to the Nazis, at that time — it was a great blessing. *(Beat.)*

The day I saw the window shade lift, a young girl's face for a moment, searching for sunlight — in that moment, I knew: The rumors are true. They are in there. You can bring them to the Nazis. You are safe. *(Beat. She remembers the moment with real pleasure, then sighs.)*

Then, of course, after the war. She has written a diary, too, hasn't she, this little girl. Well, of course she did, we all were writing. And the world embraces the scribblings of a child, this wondrous victim of so much terror. So sad, so tragic, this wasted life. And everyone, across the world, sees themselves in her youthful innocence, her hope, her despair. *(She pats the piles of paper that surround her.)*

But that is not who you are. I am dead too. But I am here. I am with you. This is who you are. This tells the story. This is what you must read. *(Fade to black.)*

END OF PLAY

THE FIRST DAY

CHARACTERS

RICK

STACEY

BARB

ALEX

PHIL

CHRISTINE

SET

Various locations around a city: a restaurant, a bar, a street, a hospital

ORIGINAL PRODUCTION

The First Day was originally produced by the 2nd Annual Boston Theater Marathon (sponsored by Boston Theatre Works) Sunday, April 18, 2000. It was directed by David Sullivan and had the following cast:

RICK . . . . .Richard Snee

STACEY . . . . .Melinda Lopez

BARB . . . . .Natalie Brown

ALEX . . . . .Vincent Siders

PHIL . . . . .John Kuntz

CHRISTINE . . . . .Andrea Walker

Rick addresses the audience. He carries two full paper bags, with handles.

RICK: The thing is, there was a moment, in my youth, when someone pointed out to me that I would be forty years old when the millennium hit. When the numbers changed to two zero zero zero, I would be 4 - 0. At the time I was barely cogent, six years old, so it was a thought that had some impact. Four zero, a number almost as large as two zero zero zero. I thought of it as something unimaginable. And now here I am. I was just six a minute ago! Sometimes I think about my own death, and I know that the next thing I know, I'll be remembering myself thinking about my death as I die.

(Lights up Stacey, who calls to him, from a table in a restaurant.)

STACEY: Rick?

RICK: Yes, here I am. Here I am.

(He goes to the table, sets the paper bags down and sits.)

STACEY: That's it? That's the stuff?

RICK: That's what they gave me.

STACEY: Oh, God.

RICK: Yeah.

STACEY: I know, I should have gone up there myself. But she was a mess, just, someone had to, and you live so close to the hospital —

RICK: He just up and died? It's so — upsetting. That something like that —

STACEY: Of course he didn't just up and die. He's been sick a long time.

RICK: He has? I didn't —

STACEY: He had it, Rick. He had It.

(She looks at him. He sits up.)

RICK: He did?

STACEY: Yes.

RICK: I didn't know.

STACEY: *(Short.)* Neither did I.

RICK: Did Barb know?

STACEY: Of course Barb knew.

RICK: But she didn't tell anybody?

STACEY: She didn't think it was anybody's business.

RICK: Of course, she's right, of course, you just — it's all so disturbing. Dying on the last day of the millennium. It's too much. Well, of course it's too much, it's the bitter end, isn't it? I'm sorry. I know I should shut up, but I'm — you know, they weren't very nice at the hospital. I was like, my friend was here, her brother died yesterday, and she forgot his stuff and they acted like, I don't know. I had to show I.D. Like, I want to spend the last day of the millennium, stealing a dead guy's stuff. Who would do that?

(Beat. They stare at the bags.)

STACEY: Fuck him.

RICK: What?

STACEY: You know how she found out he had it?

RICK: I didn't even know he had it.

STACEY: He's a major drug addict, you know?

RICK: No, I didn't know.

STACEY: So he's coming over the apartment, asking for money and stuff, which she gives him, because he's her big brother, she has always adored him, plus she doesn't want him bothering their parents, who are poor and frail and decent, and she's got diabetes, right?

RICK: Diabetes? I didn't know that either.

STACEY: So one day she's giving herself a shot of insulin and she realizes that the needle has been used. He's been sneaking back into the bathroom and shooting up with her insulin kit, while she writes him a check.

RICK: He's got AIDS, and he's using her needles?

STACEY: Yes. Without telling her.

RICK: Her own brother?

STACEY: Yes.

RICK: And they have frail parents?

STACEY: Yes.

(He looks at her, horrified, as Barb enters.)

BARB: Hi, you guys —

(Stacey and Rick leap to their feet.)

STACEY: Hi —

RICK: Hi, hi, how are you —

BARB: Oh, you know —

(She can't continue.)

RICK: I'm so sorry about your brother.

BARB: Thanks. Stacey said you were going to go up there and get his things.

RICK: Yeah.

BARB: I feel so ridiculous, having left them, but I was so — when he — it happened so — I wanted to ask, there's a friend of his, a bartender over at the West Bank who liked him a lot, but I couldn't get a hold of him, and —

RICK: I didn't mind.

BARB: Thank you.

RICK: I was happy to do it. Here.

(*He picks them up and holds them out. Barb looks at them.*)

BARB: You brought them with you?

RICK: Well, yeah.

BARB: Today? He just died yesterday, and you —

RICK: What?

STACEY: Sweetie —

BARB: (*Sobbing.*) He went so quickly.

(*She leans into Stacey and sobs.*)

RICK: OK, well, listen you guys —

STACEY: Go, go, would you go —

RICK: OK. I'll see you guys later. Happy New Year. Never mind.

(*Rick starts to go.*)

STACEY: (*Quiet.*) Rick —

(*She gestures toward the bags. Barb continues to sob.*)

RICK: What?

STACEY: Take it.

RICK: Oh. You want me to —

STACEY: Yes.

RICK: Yeah, but I —

STACEY: TAKE THE STUFF.

RICK: What should I do with it?

STACEY: Rick.

(*Rick grabs the bags and turns to the audience.*)

RICK: I don't know what makes up a life. That was a terrible story she told, him acting like that, endangering his sister's life, so recklessly? Horrible. I don't like him for it. Before, when I picked the stuff up, and I was thinking about thinking about my own death, what I could see as I glanced through the bags, the leather jacket, the filofax, it all seemed so poignant. I had very tender feelings toward these two bags. Now, I don't like them at all. They seem self involved, and sleazy. I also have to confess that my feelings might be less complicated if I didn't have a huge crush on Barb. When Stacey called and asked me to go to the hospital, I leapt at the chance, thinking this would make me something of a hero in Barb's eyes. Now I can't help but wonder if in fact Stacey, Barb's roommate, is also her lover. Did they seem like lovers to you? Is it horrible of me to be asking these obviously self-serving questions, as I travel around the city on the first day of the new millennium, carrying around

someone else's life in two brown paper bags? *(Beat.)* Listen. I don't want
you to think ill of me? But this is really not the right job for me, today.
(Lights up on Alex, a bartender.)

RICK: *(Continuing.)* So, see there was this guy, he's the brother of a friend of
mine, and he's friends, he was friends, with one of the bartenders here —
I don't know which one —

ALEX: Skinny guy? Pink hair? Not pink, but you know, he did some stuff to
his hair?

RICK: I didn't know him. All I know about him, actually, is he's, well, he dead.
And I, actually, I picked his stuff up at the hospital but I didn't really
know him, so I thought someone who did know him should keep his
stuff.

ALEX: That guy died?

RICK: Are you sure it's the same guy?

ALEX: I thought you said that's who it was.

RICK: I don't know, actually, who it was. I just know his sister.

ALEX: He had a sister?

RICK: Yeah.

ALEX: Sure, I know him.

*(He makes a gesture. Rick hands him his stuff. The bartender starts to walk
off.)*

RICK: Can you, at least, can you tell me what his name was?

ALEX: Why?

RICK: Well — you're sure it's the same guy?

ALEX: Yeah, we got high a couple times. This was an excellent guy.

RICK: Skinny, pink hair, had a sister.

ALEX: Yeah, that's the guy. What he had, he would share.

RICK: You mean he would share needles? Is that what you mean?

ALEX: Oh, man, you know what? You have a very judgmental quality to the
way you ask questions.

RICK: I'm trying to help you.

ALEX: Wrong. Wrong. You are judging. This is why — prejudice. *Judge* is the
root word of prejudice.

RICK: I'm not judging! I'm just trying — I'm trying to get through the first
day of the millennium without having my head explode.

ALEX: See? He could have helped you with that. That was the kind of thing
he knew how to take care of. In fact, you know what? I'm not gonna let
you off the hook. You need to think about who you've let yourself
become.

(He puts the bags back down in front of Rick and goes.)

RICK: I haven't become anyone. I'm not — no, no, don't — I'm sorry. I didn't mean to argue. I just wasn't sure if you knew him!

(Alex is gone. Rick is alone.)

I'm still not sure. *(Beat. He stands and thinks.)* I should just take him home, right? They'll come get him. Eventually. Barb will leave her lesbian love nest and come get her poor dead drug addicted, AIDS-infected brother. Ugh. What a terrible thing to think! I am judgmental and small minded. I'm not. I'm simply disappointed in love on the first day of the new millennium. I mean, I don't want to be insensitive, after all her brother is dead and that is very very sad but I also have to say, she led me on. Not active, well, there was some flirting, but nothing that you couldn't take back, so you can't hold that against her unless — and this is crucial — unless in fact she is a lesbian. I mean, I have not been entirely discreet about my feelings. I haven't been pushy, but there are ways in which I did in fact let them be known, so if she is a lesbian, it was, I have to say, incumbent upon her to let me know. And that is a fact. I mean, I didn't even know she was diabetic.

(Behind him, Phil, a homeless person, starts to steal the bags.)

RICK: *(Continuing.)* So, the fact is, I don't really much care about her stupid evil dead brother's stuff. In fact —

(He sees the guy stealing the stuff.)

RICK: *(Continuing.)* Hey!

PHIL: What?

RICK: That's my stuff.

PHIL: It was just sitting here.

RICK: It wasn't just sitting. I set it down.

PHIL: 'Cause you were walking over there.

RICK: Look, I don't have to explain myself. This is not your stuff! Give it back to me!

PHIL: Come on, man! Do you really need this stuff? I mean it, you need this? 'Cause I'll tell you something — I need it. Shoes and a pair of blue jeans, and a leather coat — I could really use this shit. You know?

RICK: That's not my concern.

PHIL: Oh that's really nice. You know, it's the first day of the new millennium, and you're like running around saying, I could give a shit about my fellow man. That is not good karma.

RICK: Look —

PHIL: WHAT?

(They stare at each other.)

RICK: If I give you my coat, will you give me back my stuff?

PHIL: Hand over the coat.

(He holds out his hand, makes a gesture. Rick takes off his coat, holds it out, then when Phil reaches for it, he pulls it back. Gestures toward the bags. Wary, they exchange the bags and coat. Or, perhaps there is a rolling fistfight while the stuff gets exchanged. In any event, Phil leaves the stuff and runs off with the coat. Rick sits up, looks at the audience.)

RICK: *(Beat, suddenly defensive.)* WHAT?? I had to do something! You can't just have a total stranger walking around with your stuff, after you die! I mean — SHIT. FUCK. SHIT. IT'S FUCKING COLD, AND NOW I DON'T HAVE A COAT.

(He sits for a moment, stewing, then suddenly reaches into one of the bags for the leather coat.)

RICK: *(Continuing.)* Well, I'm not gonna sit here and freeze. I'm gonna put on the damn leather jacket. The least I can get out of all this is a leather — whoa. This is nice. This lining is — whoa. *(He has the jacket on, checking it out. He puts his hands in the pockets, stops.)* Oh, wait. I shouldn't do this, right? Because who knows what's in there. Fuck. I have a hangnail. I shoved my hand right into this AIDS-infested jacket, and I HAVE A HANGNAIL. Can you get AIDS from a hangnail? Or a jacket? You can't get AIDS from a jacket, can you? FUCK!

(He yanks off the jacket and kicks the bag away from him. The stuff spills out. He tries to pick it up, then pushes it all away from him. More and more enraged.) Oh, shit. Oh FUCK. I can't think about this anymore. THIS IS CRAZY. I mean, it's obscene! This is obscene!

(Christine, a nurse, enters.)

CHRISTINE: What? I'm sorry, what did you say?

(Rick turns and starts to pack up the bags again, hands them to her.)

RICK: I have to return this dead guy's stuff. I picked it up yesterday, as a favor to a friend of mine, but now she doesn't want it, so I'm bringing it back to you.

CHRISTINE: This belongs to a patient?

RICK: He's not a patient. He's dead. And this is his stuff.

(He offers up the bags.)

CHRISTINE: What do you expect me to do with it?

RICK: GIVE. IT. BACK. TO HIM. He's still here, right? He just died yesterday, so you've still got him, right?

CHRISTINE: He's in the morgue.

RICK: Well, here's his stuff. He's going to the underworld. He's going to need it.

BARB: Rick?

(Rick turns.)

RICK: Barb. Oh. Hi.

(Christine goes. Barb looks at Rick.)

BARB: I had to come down to sign papers and things. To release the body. For the funeral.

RICK: Oh.

BARB: I'm sorry about before. Just falling apart like that.

RICK: It's all right.

BARB: I'm embarrassed. It was nice, what you did, coming down here and picking up his things. And then I just was an old crazy person.

RICK: I totally understand.

BARB: Is that his jacket?

RICK: Oh. Yeah.

(He hands it to her.)

BARB: You should keep the jacket. You need it more than I do.

RICK: No —

BARB: Why, are you afraid it's infected? *(Beat.)* Stacey told me. She told you. About what he did. I'm sorry you had to find out. 'Cause now you probably hate him.

RICK: I never met him.

BARB: No, I know, but what you know about him. That he gave it to me. My own brother. Knew he had it, and infected me.

RICK: He, he did? I wasn't sure.

(She nods, simple, sad.)

BARB: I know I should be angry. I just can't figure out how. Anyway.

(She tears up.)

RICK: Hey —

BARB: *(Getting it together.)* I'm OK. But, it does make me so sad. You know, I always thought you had kind of a crush on me. Or hoped, maybe I just hoped. And then to have to tell you that. Because that's the end of that, huh. To have dreams, just dying all around you. On the first day, of a whole millennium. I mean, I'm not giving up. I know, life is what you get. You just get what you get, and then you hope, I don't know, that it adds up to something more, that you have it in you to transcend. Or maybe not even that much, maybe you just hope that you just have it in you, through everything, to hold onto your love. I honestly don't know.

Anyway. Thank you, being such a good friend. That jacket looks really good on you. You should keep it.

(She picks up the bags, starts to go.)

RICK: Here. Give me those. I'll carry 'em for you.

BARB: I have to go to the morgue, Rick.

RICK: I'll come with you. It's time your brother and I met.

BARB: Are you sure?

RICK: Yeah. I am. You know, all of a sudden going to the morgue seems like the perfect way to start the new year.

(He picks up the bags. Grateful, she takes his arm. Lights fade.)

END OF PLAY

OFF BASE

CHARACTERS
AMANDA

JIMMY

SET
A set of bleachers

ORIGINAL PRODUCTION
Off Base was originally produced by Mile Square Theatre on June 18, 2005. It was directed by Mark Weitz with the following cast:

AMANDA . . . . .Rachel Fowler

JIMMY . . . . .Paul Haber

Amanda and Jimmy in the stands, watching a ball game. She is eating pop-corn and drinking a soda. He is much more engaged than she is. Someone hits a long drive to left field. He leaps to his feet.

JIMMY: Yes! Yes! Go go — all right. Yes!
> *(He sits. She has watched his activity and the activity on the field with a large degree of skepticism. Jimmy sits, still pumped.)*

AMANDA: You know, I was at my sister's last week, for dinner? And I was watching my niece, Florence, she's three, and you know how they have those little bottles of like bubble juice and the kids blow bubbles? And it's kind of hard for them, they can't blow too hard, or the bubbles pop right away but if they blow too soft that doesn't work either. So Florence has to really concentrate, you know, and she can do it for hours, concentrating like a motherfucker on that little bubble wand, most the time not getting a single bubble, but every now and then, you know, she would get off a huge beautiful burst of the most spectacular little bubbles. And she would smile. And you know, it was a big deal, it meant something, because she did it all by herself.

JIMMY: That's great.

AMANDA: Yeah. *(Beat.)* That's a big deal to a kid, you know. You try to help them and they go no no no, I want to do it by myself. I did, I tried to help her, and she said —

JIMMY: Yeah, OK, Amanda.

AMANDA: What.

JIMMY: Just OK, OK?

AMANDA: OK.

JIMMY: *(Calling.)* Come on Jose. Come on baby, bring it home. Come on.

AMANDA: It was so cute. "I want to do it all by myself."

JIMMY: All RIGHT.

AMANDA: What?

JIMMY: You don't want to be here, I said you don't have to come.

AMANDA: I'm not saying anything.

JIMMY: You're not saying anything.

AMANDA: I'm just telling a story about the innate moral consciousness of a three-year-old.

JIMMY: Yeah, see —

AMANDA: That's all I'm —

JIMMY: They don't all do it.

AMANDA: No, I wasn't —

JIMMY: Oh please —

AMANDA: I wasn't!

JIMMY: Sure you weren't. *(Calling.)* Inside, that was inside, come on, what is this? You suck! Get a job! Christ, did you see that?

AMANDA: No, I wasn't looking.

JIMMY: Ridiculous. *(Clapping.)* OK, let's go, let's see some action! Let's get some runs here!

AMANDA: Let's "get some runs"?

JIMMY: What am I supposed to say, "Let's get some outs"?

AMANDA: No, I just never heard that one. "Let's get some runs." I like it. *(Yelling.)* Let's get some runs!

JIMMY: OK.

AMANDA: What? I'm being enthusiastic. *(Yelling.)* Let's get some runs! Let's get some runs!

JIMMY: OK. OK.

AMANDA: You asked me to —

JIMMY: Yes, I did, and now I'm asking you to stop.

AMANDA: Fine.

(Beat. They watch the game.)

JIMMY: OK, OK, here we go. Let's go, fire up, over the fence, man! Over the fence!

AMANDA: That would be cool. If he hit it over the fence. I bet he can do it too. Look at the muscles on that guy. Wowwee zowee. He looks fantastic. You don't see that every day. I mean, even football players —

JIMMY: OKAY.

AMANDA: He must work out really hard to get muscles like that.

JIMMY: What is your problem?

AMANDA: My problem, I don't have a problem. I'm just enjoying the game, I'm enjoying watching this really buff guy try to beat the shit out of a teeny-weeny ball, without any help at all, because that's of course the moral thing to do, and baseball as we know is a completely moral game all about American values and why would you need help beating the shit out of a teeny-weeny —

JIMMY: Not all of them took steroids. Very few of them, in fact, took steroids.

AMANDA: Because that would be cheating and of course in baseball nobody cheats.

JIMMY: I never said nobody. Obviously for a few players —

AMANDA: A few!

JIMMY: A very few there was a problem, a temptation, but to act like the game itself is tainted, is just exaggerating —

AMANDA: "I'm not here to talk about the past."

JIMMY: Why should he talk about the past! It's the future of baseball that is at stake, that is —

AMANDA: You know who you remind me of? My father, after they caught Nixon. No shit, he still thinks Nixon got screwed. They had him red-handed, he betrayed not me because I was six years old, but my father, who believed in him and still believes in him and refuses to admit that he was fucking betrayed —

JIMMY: I am not anything like your father.

AMANDA: You are exactly like my father. "I wasn't betrayed. Baseball is still the holy American pastime, let's all bow down to baseball baseball baseball — "

JIMMY: Why are you so mad? What do you care?

AMANDA: Why do I care?

JIMMY: Yes, why do you —

AMANDA: Because you do this! This, this —

JIMMY: This what —

AMANDA: Willful denial. Willful —

JIMMY: Willful, there's nothing willful —

AMANDA: Deliberate —

JIMMY: Oh, I believe in the beauty of baseball and that's like a —

AMANDA: No. No. You believe in the fantasy of the beauty of baseball.

JIMMY: Baseball is beautiful.

AMANDA: It's a fucking big business run by fucking corrupt, racist, sexist bunch of capitalist creeps who take advantage of people like you, because you're idiots.

JIMMY: I'm not an idiot!

AMANDA: You are if you believe that nobody took steroids! All those home runs, you want to protect, why would you want to protect all those phony records, it makes a mockery, of of the real ones, of what Babe Ruth accomplished, and poor Roger Maris with that pathetic asterisk, he at least really hit those home runs and you want to protect —

JIMMY: They did really hit those home runs!

AMANDA: No they didn't! They cheated! They didn't do it by themselves, even a three-year-old girl knows it doesn't count if you don't do it by yourself!

JIMMY: Last I checked in America you're innocent until —

AMANDA: Jimmy —

JIMMY: You believe what you want to believe, and I'll believe what I want to believe.

AMANDA: Fine.

JIMMY: Fine. *(Beat.)* This game gives me pleasure. It gives me joy. If you don't understand that —

AMANDA: I do understand that, I'm saying why don't you fight for it!

JIMMY: I am fighting for it in the best way that I know how, by believing, by continuing to believe in the worth and the value and the exquisite possibility which is contained in the game itself. I believe in its future as well as its past which has yes at times been tainted as all life is tainted, as history is tainted, as human nature is tainted, with frailty and mistake, but which remains in its essence precious and timeless and lovely, just as the light on the field, and the roar of the crowd and the sound of the bat is all of those things. Precious. And timeless, and lovely. I believe —

AMANDA: You BELIEVE — a a a — fantasy!

JIMMY: So? SO WHAT? If the fantasy is where I want to be, why should I be in reality?

AMANDA: Because I'm here. That's why. Because I live in the real world. And I don't know how to not be real. I don't know how to lie.

JIMMY: It's not a lie.

AMANDA: They didn't take steroids. That's not a lie.

JIMMY: No. It's not.

AMANDA: *(Beat.)* You know what? I love this game as much as you do.

JIMMY: I know you do. I know that! That's what I'm saying! Sit down. Come on, Amanda. Sit down.

(She throws her popcorn in his face, and goes. He watches her go, bewildered, then, after a long moment, turns back to the game.)

JIMMY: *(Continuing.)* All right! Let's go! Let's get some runs! Let's get some runs!

(Blackout.)

END OF PLAY

MARY, MOTHER OF GOD, INTERCEDE FOR US

CHARACTERS
MARY

SET
A bare stage

ORIGINAL PRODUCTION

Mary, Mother of God, Intercede for Us was originally produced at The Rattlestick Theatre on September 20, 2006, Josh Hecht, director, with the following cast:

MARY . . . . .Bradford Louryk

Mary comes on, calling to others offstage. She carries a clipboard, with papers, which she consults.

MARY: Yes, I'll talk to him about it — I'll mention it if I have time but I have a lot of things on the docket today so it may — I know, I know — look, just take a number and — take a number. Take a number. TAKE A FUCKING NUMBER. *(Beat.)*

Sorry. I am sorry, my children, I love you all so much, every one of you is the most treasured child of my heart. I cherish the entirety of your being. You're my favorite one. All three billion of you. And how clever you all are to, you know, believe that. *(She turns back to take her place in the center of the room, smiles at God humbly.)*

Most heavenly Father I have come to you today to intercede on behalf of the many worthy Catholics who worship and adore you and pray that you may take pity on them and alleviate their sufferings in the graciousness of your everlasting wisdom and mercy, amen. *(She consults her clipboard.)*

So, in the name of your son, and mine, Christ Jesus whose sufferings on the cross redeemed us all, I won't take up too much of your time.

I have here an old lady in Queens, Louise, whose grandson is over there in Iraq, getting shot at, et cetera, by insurgents who seem pretty desperate to do him harm, because, as far as I can tell, they don't really think American soldiers belong anywhere near their cities or their oil fields, and they're pretty mad about that so they're trying to blow up this old lady's grandson, who by the way she raised him herself from the age of seven, because his mother was a crack addict, she's no longer with us, she went to the dark side, clearly, anyway, Louise raised this boy, Frankie, and he's the light of her life. She lost a lot of children to the streets but Frankie has always been a good boy, and he went into the Army because he thought that was a way to make something of himself, and now she's scared he won't come back to her and it's breaking her heart. She's really very frightened and worried; he's everything to her, and so she wants you to know about that and hopes that I can intercede on her behalf and see if you know, what you can do there for him. *(Beat. She waits for an answer. There is none.)*

So, uh, you want me to tell her anything? *(Beat.)*

I'll tell her, you know, that you feel her pain. *(Beat.)*

I feel her pain, anyway, and so I'll tell her to keep praying, that's what I'll tell her. *(She makes a note, goes to the next petition.)*

OK, this one is from Miko Obogo in Zimbabwe. You may or may not have noticed, but they've had no rain — literally none! For, well, quite a while. Quite a while, and many of them are, well, not to put too fine a point on it, they are in fact starving. To death. Miko and his wife Kalatumbe have been good Catholics for many years and they pray to you to spare the lives of their remaining two children, the youngest, Lili Namabande, she was eighteen months old, and she died last week, a rather horrible death, and they humbly ask you to well, maybe just to let it rain. A couple of good weeks of rain would end the draught and you know then there'd be food, but if that doesn't work for you they'd also appreciate it if you could manage to arrange for some of the Red Cross emergency supplies to make it through to them rather than having them all circumvented by corrupt warlords. Which I'm thinking sounds like not a bad idea, as long as you're inflicting suffering, all about, maybe you could hit that guy with you know, malaria or something. Have one of his underlings go a little crazy with ambition, stab him in the back with his bayonet. *(She demonstrates. God seems unimpressed.)*

Or there's the rain option. Whatever, obviously, works for you. *(She goes back to her list, pages through.)*

(Uncomfortable.) Oh. And then there's Sandra here, from Brazil. She has six children, living in the slums of Sao Paolo, they're very very poor, and her husband has been away working in the rain forest, doesn't say what he does there, and her brother-in-law — this is terrible — he assaulted her, unfortunately, and now she is pregnant. And she doesn't know how to tell her husband, and they clearly don't have the money for another child. And so she wants permission to have an abortion. *(Beat.)*

OK. Nevermind. I know. *(She goes on.)*

Oh, here's a good one. This one's from Theresa. She really is not someone who we hear from much, she's not a regular churchgoer by any means, in fact she more or less brags about being a "collapsed Catholic," very clever, ha ha, Theresa, anyway, Theresa has a play — *(Snide.)* — how important! She has a play opening in New York City and she's terrified that some critic from *The New York Times* is going to give it a bad review. So she'd like you to say a word to this guy — yeah, we'll get right on that, Theresa! Next . . . *(She goes down the list.)*

Oh, here's a doozy. This from Father Francis McMartin, of St. Xavier Parish in Cincinnati, Ohio. Father Francis, it seems, has been accused of doing things he shouldn't with the altar boys over there at St. Xavier Parish, and he wants you to know that he is heartily sorry —

those are his words, "heartily sorry for having offended thee," and he promises not to do it again, and begs for understanding and forgiveness and the chance to atone for his transgressions by ministering to youths in a different parish. He also would like to point out that what he did wasn't any worse than what many many people do, in the corrupt American culture, and that he was he thinks led astray by the secular media, although he admits that he may have indulged in a little too much altar wine as well, which he also regrets but which at the same time he blames for his — OK, this is his word — indiscretions. Indiscretions, that's a good one, we might also call it "raping children," how about a little forgiveness for "raping children," Father Francis, I don't think so — *(She is about to cross him off the list, then stops, looks up at God.)*

I beg your pardon? *(Beat.)*

You what? You want to have him moved to — another parish. Ah. Yes, I see. That that that, yes that was a good idea, that he had there. Let's put him in with other children, so that he can maybe rape them, too, are you crazy? Have you lost your fucking mind? *(Beat.)*

Sorry. Sorry sorry sorry. Didn't mean to have an opinion there. I'm just the woman. I'm just the mom. I should be forgiving and compassionate, you're right. Sorry for the slip there. I do, I I I sense how he's suffered and you're right he deserves another chance. *(Beat.)* Wow. OK then. OK. Let's see. What do we have, what do we have . . . *(Upset, she reads through the list for a long moment, trying to get it together.)*

You know what? That's really it for today. Nobody else is out there praying. Everything's perfect. *(Beat.)* Everything's perfect. *(Blackout.)*

END OF PLAY

DELIVER ME

CHARACTERS

PHIL

RON

SHEILA

BERNARD

LOREEN

SET

A crummy, run-down office space. There is a working sink.

ORIGINAL PRODUCTION

Deliver Me was originally produced by the 24 Hour Company as part of the 24 Hour Plays at the Atlantic Theater on March 31, 2003. It was directed by Kelley Rae O'Donnell with the following cast:

PHIL .... .Christopher Briggs

RON .... .Hugh Kelly

SHEILA .... .Louise McCabe

BERNARD .... .Matt Long

LOREEN .... .not available

(A crummy, run-down office space. The stage is empty. Offstage, there is the sound of movement, and someone mutters, pissed.)

PHIL: *(Grunting.)* Fuck. Motherfucking mother fucker. *(The sound of something banging into the wall.)*

RON: *(Grunting.)* Fuck.

PHIL: *(Overlap.)* Owww. Fucking, would you fucking—
(More sounds of banging.)

RON: *(Overlap.)* Fuck! Fuck! Fuck!

PHIL: *(Overlap.)* Stop, stop, fucking, would you fucking stop?
(More sounds of banging.)

RON: STOP. STOP. STOP.

PHIL: Fuck!
(The sounds stop. After a moment, Phil appears in the doorway, out of breath. He looks around, unhappy.)

PHIL: *(Continuing.)* Fuck, forget it, this is fucked.
(Ron appears behind him, checks out the doorway.)

RON: Fuck! I mean, this is—

PHIL: I know—
(He starts to dial the phone on the desk.)

RON: It stinks in here. What a dump. I hate these old buildings. Why doesn't somebody blow this place up, they're all so interested in blowing up the fucking city all of a sudden, why don't they fucking blow up these fucking bullshit crummy old dumps? That's what I would do. Fuck. I think I broke my fucking hand.

PHIL: *(On phone.)* Hey it's me. Look, we got the desk over here, Frank, and there's a problem.

RON: *(Overlap.)* There's no one even here. I mean, that's fucked. This is the right address, right? Fuck.

PHIL: *(Overlap, on phone, excruciatingly polite.)* Well, it's pretty big, as you'll recall, and we can't even get it to the landing. Yeah, but that's not — no, listen to me. This is, no, don't send — I, I respect and appreciate that, but I don't think it's going to help, Frank —

RON: *(Overlap.)* Who's he want to send? Is he talking about sending that fucking Bernard over here? That's just what we fucking need, fucking waste-of-time piece-of-shit Bernard. Tell him we don't want Bernard.

PHIL: *(Overlap.)* I'm not kidding, it's not going to matter how many guys are here to move it. It's a matter of the dimensions, Frank, and that's why I think that Bernard is — listen to me, Frank — Frank — . *(Beat. Frank seemingly has hung up on him.)* And fuck you too, you fucking shithead. YOU FUCK, YOU FUCKING FUCKER!

(He hangs up the phone.)

RON: Is he sending that fuckhead shithead Bernard?

PHIL: He's calling him.

RON: FUCK.

PHIL: Would you shut up? I mean, would you just fucking shut up for three seconds so I can think about this here?

RON: He's going to kill you, if we don't get that thing in here. I mean, Frank is already, after last week?

PHIL: That wasn't my fault. I TOLD HIM —

RON: I know, I know, I'm just saying, Frank is gonna kill you. I think my fucking hand is broken.

(Ron looks at the sink, looks at his hand. Phil looks at the delivery slip, worried. Ron turns on the sink, jumps when water comes out.)

RON: *(Continuing.)* Whoa! Look at that! Fuck! Phil! Look at this!

PHIL: What?

RON: There's a sink in the middle of the room, and it works. These fucking old dumps are amazing, aren't they?

(He sticks his hand under the water. Offstage, Sheila suddenly can be heard.)

SHEILA: FUCK.

(There is the sound of scrambling, more cursing. Ron turns the water off.)

SHEILA: *(Continuing.)* What the fuck is this? Fuck me. Fucking — ow, Jesus Mary and Joseph, Jesus fucking Christ —

(She falls onto the steps behind the open office doorway. She wears a very short skirt and high heels, considerable makeup, hair poofed and set. She pulls herself to her feet, yanks her skirt down, and hobbles into the office.)

SHEILA: *(Continuing.)* What the fuck is going on here? There's a fucking desk the size of a BUICK in the middle of the stairwell! I had to fucking climb over it to even get here! I mean, what the fuck, that thing is a fucking BOAT! I had to fucking CLIMB OVER — shit, I broke a nail. I broke a — shit shit shit — *(She goes into the bathroom, to check her hair out.)* And there better not be a run in these or I swear on the tomb of the lord Jesus Christ himself that I will sue SOMEBODY, I don't know who, but — Oh God! There is, there's a run! There's a run in my Goddamn stockings! It's not even ten AM, and this day is totally fucked! Who the FUCK left a fucking desk in the middle of the fucking stairwell?

PHIL: You Sheila?

SHEILA: Yeah, who the fuck are you?

PHIL: We're the fucking delivery guys, and that would be your fucking desk.
(*He holds up the delivery slip, waves it at her. She looks at them, suspicious, but she hobbles back out into the hallway. After a moment, Sheila comes back in.*)

SHEILA: It didn't look that big in the store.

PHIL: It's a pretty big desk.

SHEILA: Yes, well, you can just — bring it in here, then. It goes right here. So maybe if we moved this desk out of the way, first —

PHIL: It's not going to happen.

SHEILA: But you just said —

PHIL: Even if we get it over the top of the stairwell? Which is, that thing weighs a lot, I don't know how much —

RON: A lot.

PHIL: It won't go through the doorway. It's the dimensions, the dimensions are off.

SHEILA: The dimensions?

PHIL: Did you check the dimensions, before you bought it? I mean, did you measure the doorway and stuff?

SHEILA: *(Lying.)* Of course I did.

PHIL: *(Knows that was a lie.)* Well, I don't know what to tell you, Sheila. The desk can't go up the stairs, it can't make it around the turn at the top of the stairs, and it can't fit through the doorway. So maybe your measuring tape was, you know. Flawed, or something. The desk is too big.

SHEILA: That's what he wanted. My boss. He wanted a big, nice desk. Antiques. You know. He thinks it'll make the place look nice.

RON: This place?

SHEILA: That's what he said! Buy me some fucking nice furniture so this place doesn't look like such a fucking dump!

RON: This place needs more than nice furniture. This place needs to be blown up. But the sink is nice, that's a nice touch.

SHEILA: Look, you guys, I know you don't have to, and I'm sorry about the dimensions, but trust me, we got to get that thing in here.

PHIL: It won't go through the doorway.

RON: He's right. It's too big. *(Beat.)* It's just too big.

SHEILA: Could you. . . I mean, huh. *(Taking a breath.)* Hooo. Huh.

PHIL: You OK?

SHEILA: Oh yeah, it's not a problem. Not a problem, not a problem.
(*But she is hyperventilating. Out in the hall, another voice is heard yelling.*)

LOREEN: *(Offstage.)* THERE'S A FUCKING DESK OUT HERE —
WHO THE FUCK — FUUUUCKKK —
(Another young woman, Loreen, falls over the desk, into the doorway. She staggers in.)

LOREEN: There's a desk the size of Alaska out here.

SHEILA: *(Upset.)* THAT'S WHAT HE SAID HE WANTED, HE SAID
HE WANTED IT BIG.
(Beat.)

PHIL: Look, Sheila — you need to take responsibility for this.

SHEILA: What? I need to what?

PHIL: You need to sign the slip, that you refused delivery. We'll take it back
to the store, you exchange it for a smaller desk, we bring it back out next
week.

SHEILA: Next week is too late.

PHIL: We can't get it through the door, Sheila.

SHEILA: You haven't even tried! I don't refuse delivery! You get it in here!

PHIL: I can't get it in here!

SHEILA: It's your job!

PHIL: My job was to get it as far as I could get it! I got it to the stairwell. You
want me to leave it there, I can do that for you.

RON: Frank is going to kill you if you —

PHIL: Would you shut up?

SHEILA: I don't take responsibility! I don't! Is it my responsibility, my boss
is a teeny-dick nut-job shithead who thinks bad antiques are going to get
him laid? In this office? This hideous ugly office with dirty brown wall-
paper and the worst bathroom in America, this place looks like a slum,
and it smells, because he doesn't take a bath, the guy doesn't bathe and
every day I come in here and just want to puke with how bad it smells
and how pathetic it is, and how repulsive he is and what happened to
my life, why am I hanging onto this horrible job, but I'm scared, you
know, scared shitless because they keep telling me how bad the
economy is and so I do whatever crazy thing he tells me, I went out there
and bought him a ridiculous, ridiculously beautiful desk, because — oh
because I don't know why. He is like the worst human being I have ever
met, why do I do things for him? Why does he get that pretty desk? Why
are those the people who get to be the boss? Why?

PHIL: I don't know.

SHEILA: I don't know either. So how is this my responsibility, you shithead?

It's your responsibility to get that fucking desk in here! I am not losing my job!

PHIL: Well, I'm not losing my job!

SHEILA: Fuck you.

PHIL: Fuck you too!

(Out in the hallway, there is another voice.)

BERNARD: *(Offstage.)* Fuck. I mean, whoa, fuck! Hey — fuck!

RON: Oh, shit.

PHIL: Shit.

LOREEN: Who's that?

(There are more sounds of someone climbing, and Bernard comes careening into the doorway. He is young and handsome and feckless.)

BERNARD: Whoa! Wow! That thing is huge! It's Mount Everest! You could go fucking skiing on that thing!

RON: Hey, Bernard.

BERNARD: *(Happy.)* Hey! Fuck! Frank called and said you were kind of fucked over here, and from what I see that is the fucking truth. I mean, that thing is stuck! Tight as a drum. I did a little dance on it, and it's just packed down into the turn of the stairwell out there, like a fucking sardine in a fucking tuna can or something. Beautiful piece of furniture, too. I mean, that is a desk for fucking Zeus, or fucking someone fucking great, isn't it? And it's not going forward or backward, it's just stuck out there. Stuck in the stairwell. Unless the building burns down, we are alllll fucked. *(He laughs, happily, he thinks this is hilarious.)* I'm sorry. I know I'm an idiot. I don't know what to tell you. Fire. Fire! Fiiiire! Why not? Why the fuck not? I just think that would be really funny.

(Sheila and Phil look at each other. The lights come down as the flames go up. Blackout.)

END OF PLAY